Vegan
Microwave
Cookbook

Also by Nancy Berkoff, RD

Vegan Passover Recipes—
Eggless & Dairy-free Dishes

Vegan Meals for One or Two—
Your Own Personal Recipes

Vegan in Volume—
Vegan Quantity Recipes for Every Occasion

Dedication

Vegan Microwave Cookbook is dedicated to Bob, who let me smoke up his microwave, singe his cooking turntable, and devise frightening meal combinations in the name of nutrition. To Bob, who ministered to my computer and insisted on a policy of "back up often." For all his general wonderfulness, I promise a lifetime of happiness (and no more quinoa-bean loaves).

Vegan Microwave Cookbook

By Chef Nancy Berkoff, RD

The Vegetarian Resource Group
Baltimore, Maryland

A Note to the Reader
The contents of this book and our other publications, including web information, are not intended to provide personal medical advice. Medical advice should be obtained from a qualified health professional. We often depend on product and ingredient information from company statements. It is impossible to be 100% sure about a statement, information can change, people have different views, and mistakes can be made. Please use your own best judgement about whether a product is suitable for you. To be sure, do further research or confirmation on your own.

© Copyright 2003, The Vegetarian Resource Group
PO Box 1463, Baltimore, MD 21203.

Cover artwork by Lance Simons
Illustrations by Rowen Leigh

Library of Congress Cataloging-in-Publication Data

Berkoff, Nancy.
  Vegan microwave cookbook / by Nancy Berkoff.
      p. cm.
Includes index.
  ISBN 0-931411-26-2
  1. Vegan cookery. 2. Microwave cookery. I. Title.
  TX837.B477623 2003
  641.5'636--dc21

                                    2003010890

Printed in the United States of America

10 9 8 7 6 5 4 3 2 1

Table of Contents

Preface..9

Introduction..10
    If You Can Boil Water, You Can Cook with
       a Microwave...10
    "What?" You Say, "Cook Nutritious Food
       in a Microwave? Food Even My Friends
       Will Enjoy?"..10
    How Do Microwaves Work?............................11
    Microwave Cooking Terms.............................12
    Tips for Getting the Most Out of Your
       Microwave..14
    Microwave Cooking Times..............................14
    The Dish Test...15
    The Power of It All...15
    The Right Dish for the Right Job......................16
    Microwave Cover Up.......................................16
    Microwave Don'ts..17
    Turn, Turn, Turn...18

Chapter 1: Shopping and Stocking..........................19
    Introduction..19
    Buying the Microwave.....................................19
    Microwave Safety..21
    Pots and Pans..22
    Storing Leftovers...23
    Cleaning the Microwave..................................24
    Stocking the Pantry and Refrigerator..............25
    More Food for Thought....................................25
    Overall Kitchen Safety.....................................30

TABLE OF CONTENTS CONTINUED

Chapter 2: Vegan Menu Planning.............................. **32**
  Introduction.. 32
  Basic Information for Daily Vegan Meal
      Planning.....................................36
  Sample Menu.....................................38
  Microwave Meal Planning............................. 39
  Microwave Creativity............................... 40
  More Ideas for Vegan Microwave Meals........ 42

**Chapter 3: Converting Traditional Recipes to the
  Microwave**...**45**
  Introduction.. 45
  How to Select Recipes to Convert...................46
  Selecting Microwave Cooking from
      Conventional Methods............................ 47
  Estimating Time and Testing for Doneness... 48
  Ingredient Tips.....................................48
  Baking in the Microwave.............................50
  Ingredients that Don't Work.........................51
  How to Use this Chapter.............................52
  Soups... 52
  Hot Sandwiches......................................55
  Casseroles...56
  Baked Goods and More............................... 62

Chapter 4: Microwave Baking and Desserts......................**68**
  Introduction..68
  Ideas for Preparing Hot Desserts When You
      Don't Have Time to Make Them from
      Scratch..69
  Microwave Baking Techniques....................... 70
  Sauces and Toppings............................... 72
  Quick Breads.......................................76
  Muffins and Pies...................................84

Pie Fillings...92
Puddings and Hot Fruit........................94
Biscuits and More................................ 99
Bars and Fudge..................................104

Chapter 5: Entrées: Medleys, Curries, and Casseroles.... 106
Introduction....................................... 106
How to "Build a Meal" Around an Entrée...106
Loaves and "Meat" Balls.....................107
Some Microwave Cooking Tips for "Meat"
    Balls..108
Basic "Meat" Ball Recipe Variations.............109
Cooking Pasta.................................... 110
Recipes...111

Chapter 6: Microwave Appetizers and Side Dishes........ 136
Pointers to Make Your Life Easier................. 137
Recipes...139

Chapter 7: Microwave Soups, Dips, and Dressings.........174
Introduction....................................... 174
From-Scratch Soups Versus "Open and Go"175
Microwave-Soaking Dried Beans and
    Legumes..176
Vegetable Stock.................................. 177
From Scratch Soups............................ 178
Soups to Serve Warm..........................182
Soups to Serve Cold............................186
Dips and Salad Dressings....................191

Chapter 8: Microwave Breakfast and Hot Beverages.......197
Some A.M. Microwave Tips........................... 197
Recipes...199

TABLE OF CONTENTS CONTINUED

**Appendix 1: The Perfectly Stocked Microwave
   Kitchen**..**218**
   Tools of the Trade................................218
   In Addition to the Microwave......................218
   A Little More Detail..............................219
   Microwave Equipment Bells and Whistles.. 220
   Cookware.. 221
   Thoughts on Stocking the Pantry.................. 223

Appendix 2: Vegan Glossary....................................**224**

**Appendix 3: More Microwave Vegan Menus:
   Suggestions and Recipes for Holidays, Parties, and
   Entertaining**...**232**
   Menu Ideas...................................... 233
   Recipes.. 236
   Passover Microwave Recipes........................ 247

Appendix 4: Microwave Maven...............................**254**
   Fast Microwave Guide............................. 257
   Using Leftovers.................................. 260

The Vegetarian Resource Group Catalog.................... 263

Index By Subject.. 272
Index By Recipe...274
Index By Major Ingredient.......................................278

ACKNOWLEDGMENTS
Thanks to Eben Packwood, David Herring, MS, RD, and Susan Petrie for proofreading the manuscript and making suggestions. A big thanks to Debra Wasserman for editing and laying out the entire book. Thanks to Sarah Ellis, MS, RD, for providing the nutritional analyses for each recipe.

Preface

Fast, easy, good-tasting, exciting, comforting. Words that describe what people want from their meals. Words that decribe microwave cooking.

Just about everyone would like to come home to a pot of soup that's been slowly simmering on the stove all day. Or wake up to hot muffins in the morning. However, unless you have an enchanted kitchen, these dream dishes are probably not going to materialize unless you become acquainted with your microwave. Your microwave holds the secret to any type of meal you desire: comforting, indulgent, holiday, ethnic, nutritious, and fun. You and your microwave can form a great team. You shop and chop, your microwave will steam and stew.

Many of the recipes in this book will take under 10 minutes to cook. The preparation time will vary depending on your kitchen skills and the form in which you purchase your ingredients. For example, pre-shredded carrots cost a bit more than whole carrots, but they save you time. You'll decide, based on your schedule and your budget.

Preparing microwave meals will allow you to have more "home-cooked" meals. No longer will there be excuses for grabbing a fast food nosh. The extra 15 minutes you took to wait on line at a restaurant is about the amount of time you need to prepare a great meal at home. Microwave cooking is fast and offers instant gratification.

You'll find a variety of recipes in this book. Some are best for busy school or work mornings or night, others are good for entertaining. Many take advantage of seasonal ingredients and some are perfect for eating now and freezing some for later. Whatever your life style and your cooking space, you'll find recipes that will fit your microwave cooking desires.

Introduction

If You Can Boil Water, You Can Cook with a Microwave!
We'll start with the easy part. Once you know how to boil water in your microwave, you can estimate the heating time for foods, and you can make yourself a fast cup of tea or instant coffee to boot.

A general rule of thumb for microwaves is that about 1 cup (8 ounces) of water should boil in 2-3 minutes on HIGH. So, test it out. Fill a microwaveable cup or glass that holds 8 ounces with cool tap water. Place it in the center of the microwave and set the microwave for 3 minutes on HIGH. Now watch. See how long it takes for the water to come to a boil. Now you know!

If you use a lower power, like MEDIUM, then it will probably take twice as long, about 6 minutes, to boil water. If you use twice as much water, 2 cups, then it should take twice as long or 6 minutes on HIGH. You get the idea; read on.

"What?" You Say, "Cook Nutritious Food in a Microwave? Food Even My Friends Will Enjoy?"
Yes, not only is it possible, but it's also quick, requires less clean-up than traditional cooking methods, and in some cases, can actually retain more nutrients in the foods you cook.

Learning to cook with a microwave takes a little time, a little effort, and a little concentration. Just as you learned how your traditional oven works, you'll "evolve" with your microwave.

Depending on your menu, you may prepare an entire meal in your microwave or may use it as an integral part of your cooking assemblage to free up an extra burner or part of the oven. If you have limited kitchen space, or no kitchen space, the microwave can be your link to varied cooked meals.

The recipes in this book may contain a little more information than conventional recipes. Because we want to take as much guess work out as possible, we've included more details than simply saying "cook on high." Take the time to read through the recipes so you're familiar with the instructions before you start. After a short time, you'll know how your microwave cooks various foods and will be able to select the best settings for the most uniform cooking.

Many of the recipes in this book take 15 minutes or less for kitchen preparation and less than 10 minutes to cook. Some actually take only 15 minutes from the start of preparation to the commencement of eating.

You don't have to be vegan to enjoy these recipes. If you simply want to trim calories, you'll like microwave cooking. You don't need to grease the pan, since foods don't stick. You can sauté in a few drops of water or stock, instead of oil or margarine. You can steam wonderfully without any extra contraptions in your microwave. It's also easy to microwave single portions, so you can cut down on leftovers (or overeating). Some foods are thought to retain more nutrients in the microwave. This could be due to the retention of natural fluids and reduced cooking time.

How Do Microwaves Work?
Microwaves (the waves themselves, not the ovens) are attracted to molecules that are made of water and ingredients that contain water, such as fat and natural sugars. Microwaves induce water-containing ingredients to vibrate

at a very fast rate, causing friction. The friction translates into heat. In other words, microwaves get water molecules so excited that they bump into each other at a faster and faster rate until they become very hot. This event is similar to rubbing two sticks together until you create fire.

Microwaves can penetrate approximately 3/4 to 1-1/2 inches into food. Believe it or not, microwaves cook from the outside in, not from the inside out. The heat from the outer edges of food is conducted into the interior. The heat is trapped inside and the heated molecules vibrate their way back out. Those dancing water molecules that have been heating while your microwave oven is on will continue to heat for about 2-3 minutes after the microwave oven is turned off. This is important to note for two reasons:

1. You need to let microwaved food sit for a moment or two after the oven has been turned off to allow steam to dissipate, or you'll get burned.
2. You'll want to be careful not to over cook microwaved food. Since it's not browning or forming a crust, there is a tendency to think food is not finished cooking.

Keep in mind also that microwaves are reflected, not absorbed by metal. This is why metal cooking equipment is not used in microwaves.

Microwave Cooking Terms

Arrange: placing food on a platter or in a cooking dish so it will cook evenly. This usually means placing food in a circle with thicker pieces facing towards the outside of the cooking dish.

Elevate: for more efficient heating, some recipes will ask you to elevate a cooking dish. This can be done with a microwave-safe rack.

Hot Spot: your microwave may have an area in which more energy is concentrated. To test for a hot spot, place sliced white bread across the bottom of your microwave, so that the slices are touching, forming a solid layer. Microwave on HIGH for 5 minutes. If the bread shows any brown spots, these are indications of hot spots. You'll know how to arrange food in your microwave to either avoid or take advantage of hot spots.

Microwave Cookware: glass, ceramic, or plastic cookware (bowls, plates, casseroles, etc.) that are sold as microwave-safe. Some cookware are designed to be used in both conventional and microwave cooking. Be certain to check your cookware and to follow instructions for use.

Oven Cooking Bags: some markets sell transparent bags designed specifically for conventional or microwave cooking. Do not use plastic bags, storage bags, sandwich bags, or any other type of bag not specifically made for microwave cooking.

Rotate: turn a cooking dish 1/4 to 1/2 turn after having cooked in a microwave oven for a period of time. This better assures even cooking.

Turntable: some microwaves come with a built in turntable. You may purchase a turntable as an accessory if your microwave does not have one. If your microwave has a turntable, you do not need to rotate cooking dishes.

Tips for Getting the Most Out of Your Microwave
1. Your microwave must have its own electrical socket.
If your microwave shares a circuit with other appliances,
it may cook more slowly than recipes indicate.

2. Be certain that your microwave is plugged into a
3-pronged, grounded outlet.

3. Never use an extension cord for a microwave, not even
an industrial-strength one.

Microwave Cooking Times
Most foods cook in 6-7 minutes per pound on HIGH. Foods
that are higher in fat, like soymilk or peanut butter, cook
faster. The recipes in this book were written for an 800-1000
watt microwave. Cooking times will differ, depending on
the wattage and the efficiency of your microwave (see #1 in
Tips for Getting the Most Out of Your Microwave). If your
microwave is 600-700 watts, add about 20% to the cooking
time. For a 500-600 watt oven, add about 33% more time.

If you double a recipe, expect to add 50% more cooking
time and if you halve a recipe expect to subtract 33% from
the cooking time.

If you have a recipe for preparing one item, and you
would like to cook four of that same item, expect to add
triple the cooking time. For example, if a recipe for one
baked potato calls for 1 minute on HIGH, then cooking four
baked potatoes will require 3 minutes.

Extra liquid adds more cooking time, so if you add extra
liquid to a recipe, add more cooking time. Also, foods cook
quicker when spread out in a shallow plate or casserole.

Fresher fruits and vegetables tend to cook quicker than
those that are older. Dry ingredients, such as rice, quinoa,
and oats, take almost the same time to cook in the micro-

wave as they do conventionally. In a microwave, however, you can cook and store them in the same dish.

The Dish Test

You may have a favorite dish that you would like to use in the microwave, but you're not certain if it is microwave-safe. There's a method to find out. Measure 1/2 cup cold water into a glass cup. Place the glass cup and your dish side by side in microwave. Microwave on HIGH for 1 minute. If the water in the cup is hot and the dish is cool or slightly warm then the dish is safe. If the dish is hot, don't use it in a microwave. Never use anything you think contains metal in the microwave. It's generally a good idea to avoid using handpainted dishware in the microwave, too.

The Power of It All

Here is a fast guide to the most common settings:

HIGH: this will be the setting you use to cook most foods, such as fresh or frozen vegetables, grains, soups, and fruit. Most foods, unless they are very delicate, can be reheated on HIGH.

MEDIUM HIGH: is about 70% of HIGH and is good for slow cooking, cooking dense foods such as mashed potatoes, or reheating delicate dishes such as a tofu-cream pasta casserole.

MEDIUM: is about 50% of HIGH and is good to develop flavors, break down tough textures, and to prevent burning. Cream sauces or melting chocolate are done on MEDIUM.

DEFROST or MEDIUM-LOW: is about 30% of HIGH and is good for defrosting frozen vegetables, to simmer soups, or to soften foods such as margarine.

The Right Dish for the Right Job

- Use deep glass bowls for soups and sauces or rice and potatoes.
- Glass measuring cups are good for cooking soups, sauces, and gravies.
- You can use traditional tandoors (clay bakers) in a microwave. Soak tandoors in water for at least 15 minutes before using.
- Deep round casseroles with a lid can be used for casseroles and beans.
- A microwave-safe roasting rack is important for roasting potatoes and vegetables and for elevating dishes for more even cooking.
- Shallow casseroles are good for foods cooked in a single layer, such as corn-on-the-cob, baked tofu, or broccoli spears.
- Straight-sided dishes and casseroles allow for more even heating. Sometimes a slope-sided dish can give you overcooked edges.

Microwave Cover Up

Microwave recipes will sometimes instruct you to cover dishes when cooking. This is to retain moisture and heat. It also helps to keep the food in the dish, and off the walls of your microwave.

Try to have some microwave dishes and casseroles with fitting lids. If you don't have lids, you can use microwave-safe plastic wrap. Always leave one corner half an inch open to vent. If you want to, you can insert a wooden chopstick through the plastic wrap, so you can stir foods without having to remove the plastic wrap.

Parchment paper and waxed paper can be used when a loose covering is needed. Never use plastic or paper grocery bags or other plastic in the microwave. They could catch on fire or some of their components could leach into the food.

If a food has its own natural covering, such as a potato, it needs to be vented to allow steam to escape. Do this by piercing evenly with a fork or a knife.

Microwave Don'ts

1. Don't attempt to bake yeast breads in a microwave. A conventional oven will produce a far better product.

2. Don't use cracked or chipped dishes or cups in a microwave. They can shatter while cooking.

3. Microwaves can't be used for canning. Temperatures do not stay elevated long enough to make homemade foods safe to store.

4. Don't turn your microwave on when it is empty. If your microwave collects steam from cooking, leave the door open and wipe out the steam.

5. Don't use your microwave as a dryer or a warmer. Socks don't belong in the microwave, just like a cup of coffee doesn't belong in the dryer.

6. Don't use single-use paper or plastic products more than once. They can burn, catch on fire, or release toxic substances into the food.

7. Never use styrofoam or plastic take-home containers in a microwave.

Turn, Turn, Turn

We have included very few directions for rotating containers in the recipes. It is assumed that the dishes are being cooked on a turntable. If you don't have a turntable, you need to rotate the containers manually to get even cooking. You will see a few recipes that give directions for rotating containers. This is in addition to the regular turntable action. Some heat sensitive recipes, especially microwave baking recipes, require very even heat distribution. Additional rotation assists with this. If your microwave does not have a built-in turntable, you have two options:

1. Visit a kitchen appliance store and purchase a portable microwave turntable. These can be placed in your microwave when you need them. They usually work on a spring mechanism. You wind them up, just like a child's toy top, and put them in your microwave where they'll rotate for 3-5 minutes.

2. You can manually rotate the cooking container. It means you would need to stop the microwave, turn the container 1/4 turn, and resume cooking. This means you'll have to locate yourself close to the microwave and remember which way you turned the container. You should rotate a container at least once a minute.

CHAPTER ONE
Shopping and Stocking

Introduction

Depending on the space you have for food preparation, you may be using microwave cooking as your primary method of cooking or as a supplement to preparing dishes with a stove and oven. Microwaves do not have open flames and give off less heat than stoves and ovens. When preparing some types of food, cooking time may be decreased when using a microwave.

You do not need a lot of equipment or ingredients, but you'll need a small supply of each. The following should be a helpful guide as you set up to cook in your microwave.

Buying the Microwave

The number of people you will be cooking for, your eating habits and lifestyle, and the space you have available should all be considerations when buying your microwave. If you buy one that is too big, you could be wasting space and electricity. If you buy one that is too small, you may have to cook one item in several batches to prepare sufficient quantities. We do not recommend purchasing second-hand microwaves, unless they have never been uncrated and still have a warranty and safety certificate.

You can buy a full-size, mid-size, or small microwave with different wattage. Your microwave should be large enough to hold your favorite casserole dish. Many microwaves offer variable power settings, such as HIGH, MEDIUM HIGH, and DEFROST. Some smaller models have only one power setting. If you select a microwave with variable power levels, you'll be able to do more with it.

Find a reputable manufacturer when purchasing your microwave and make sure it comes with a good warranty, covering all mechanical and electrical parts for at least one year. Check to be sure that your microwave is approved by UL or NSF or other nationally recognized safety agencies. If store personnel don't have this information, do some research on the Web or go to another store!

We think an automatic turntable in a microwave is very important, but some people will say you lose space in the oven. One way or another, foods will have to be rotated several times during the cooking process. You will have to make a decision if you want to rotate food by hand (which involves stopping the microwave and rotating the dish or plate), or if you are willing to sacrifice several inches of interior space for an automatic turntable. If you already own a microwave that doesn't have a turntable, you can purchase a separate turntable. A separate turntable usually needs to be wound up before each use, working on a spring principle rather than being electrically powered.

Microwave ovens come in all shapes and sizes, with every type of bell and whistle. The recipes in this book were written for a basic microwave, 800-1000 watts, with an automatic turntable. Some microwaves offer convection, broiling (or browning), and combination cycles.

The convection cycle is like cooking in a regular gas or electric oven, with hot air circulated by a fan supplying the heat. Convection cycles are designed to provide a crisp, brown exterior to foods. Items such as pizza, cookies, muffins, and French fries crisp and form crusts in the convection cycle. If you do purchase a microwave with a convection cycle, be sure to allow the microwave to cool down between use of the convection and the microwave cycles. Be very careful not to burn yourself when removing foods from the microwave when they have been cooked with the convection cycle.

A broil cycle on a microwave usually heats foods from 400-450 degrees, not quite as hot as a conventional oven, but much hotter than a typical microwave. Broiling in a microwave will take longer than in a conventional oven, as the heat is not as strong in a microwave. Be very careful not to burn yourself while removing foods from the microwave when you have been using the broil cycle.

A combination cycle alternates between microwave and convection cycles, usually with a preprogrammed timer. Combination cooking allows foods to retain maximum fluid internally while browning on the outside. Foods are juicier and shrink less than when cooked conventionally. You'll have to convert the times called for in your recipes when using this cycle. Times are usually reduced by 1/2 or 1/4. It will take a bit of practice to learn how to use this cycle.

A sensor attachment will stop the cooking when the food reaches a certain temperature or humidity level. The sensor is usually a probe inserted into the food while it cooks in the microwave. If you buy a sensor, read the directions carefully for its proper use, cleaning, and storage.

Microwave Safety
Before you purchase your microwave, measure the spot where you'll be putting it. Be sure you can dedicate an electrical plug to the microwave. Never use an extension cord. Always make sure your microwave is plugged into a grounded 3-pronged outlet and never remove the third or grounding prong from the microwave plug.

If possible, you may want to dedicate an entire electrical circuit or fuse to your microwave. If your microwave shares a circuit with other appliances and these appliances are in use at the same time as your microwave, you will have a slower microwave cooking time. Shared or not, be certain your microwave is placed so that it can vent. Be sure to note where the vents are on the outside of your microwave. Situate the microwave so that the vents have clearance and hot air can escape from the microwave.

Kitchen fires that begin inside the microwave are very rare. If this does happen in your kitchen, do not open the microwave. Shut off the oven and pull out the plug, if possible. Cover the vents with a heavy towel to block the flow of oxygen. Do not attempt to open the door until you are certain the fire is out.

Pots and Pans
Once you have decided upon the type of foods you are going to prepare, you can decide on the plastic and glass-ware you are going to purchase.

Glass has the advantage of transferring from the micro-wave to a conventional oven. You may want to start a dish in the microwave and finish it in the oven or vice versa. Plastic is thinner and may reduce cooking times. Whichever material you decide on, do check that it is microwave-safe.

Deep casserole dishes or casseroles with high sides are versatile. They can be used in the microwave to prepare soups, casseroles, vegetables, sauces, and baked goods. One-, two-, and three-quart casseroles with lids are very useful for heavy duty microwave cooking.

You can microwave in bowls, cups, or even square con-tainers. Assess your daily needs and have on hand 2-3 of the most popular size cooking containers. For example, if you think your usual evening meal will consist of a "big" dish, like a pasta or a bean and vegetable casserole, and two side dishes, be sure you have a 2-quart casserole for the "big" dish and two smaller glass bowls for the side dishes. If you think you might be microwaving a soup while you're eating your meal, then you'll want a second 2-quart casserole. (See Appendix One for more details on selecting microwave cookware and accessories.)

You will want to find as many bowls or casseroles with lids as possible. As stated earlier, if lids are not available, you can use plastic wrap or waxed paper. The type of food you are cooking will determine which material you will use. On occasion, use paper towels, dampened paper towels, or clean, thin kitchen towels to cover microwaved foods. Recipes will give you directions on this. Covering microwaved dishes helps to retain moisture and nutrients and to reduce cooking times.

Many types of dishes and bowls are microwave-safe. Check labels or contact manufacturers to verify. Also, see Appendix One for more information.

Storing Leftovers
Microwaved leftovers should be stored just as any other perishable food is in your kitchen. This means storing foods in the refrigerator or freezer, in airtight containers or kitchen bags. Label and date your leftovers so you can plan meals with them or discard them when they are past a safe eating date. Leftover foods with ingredients such as tofu, tempeh, seitan, fake meats, vegan cheese or yogurt, beans, and vegan milk should be frozen immediately or should be refrigerated for no more than two days. You might want to invest in a refrigerator and freezer thermometer. Your refrigerator should be less than 40 degrees Fahrenheit and your freezer right around 0 degrees Fahrenheit.

You can store foods right in the container you used to microwave them. Be sure they have a fitted lid or are tightly covered with plastic wrap.

Cleaning the Microwave

Your microwave requires cleaning on a regular basis for food safety and aesthetics. Remember, if there is any spilled food on the walls or floor of the microwave, it will cook whenever the microwave is used. You don't want to be scouring twice-baked sweet potato mush off the walls of your microwave. Food can burn in the microwave. Small amounts of food stuck to the microwave's wall will burn very quickly, giving off a bad aroma and becoming more and more difficult to clean.

You can moisten a cloth, add a drop of liquid dish detergent, and heat on HIGH for 15 seconds. (We know, we told you not to run an empty microwave, but this is safe.) Now you've got a hot cloth to clean with; good for cleaning the microwave and other areas of your kitchen.

Be sure to keep the turntable and the door seal clean; they can get spatters of food on them as well. Don't use scouring pads, abrasive cleaners, or ammonia on a microwave. If you still have the manufacturer's booklet, look up the suggestions made for microwave cleaning. If you keep your microwave clean all the time, you won't need any heavy duty cleaning techniques.

Microwaves can accumulate odors. You may want to make a cinnamon rice pudding, but the microwave still has remnants of garlic eggplant; not a great combination! Here's a solution: mix 2 cups of water with 1/2 cup lemon juice in a glass cup. Microwave on HIGH for 8 minutes. Or you can measure 1/2 cup vinegar into a glass cup and microwave on HIGH for 1-1/2 minutes. These solutions should help absorb your microwave's unwanted odors.

Stocking the Pantry and the Refrigerator

There are many ways to plan for a balanced diet, vegan or not. (See Chapter Two for details on vegan meal planning.) The key is in variety. And variety should hopefully come easy; few people are happy with a monotonous diet. Does this mean that you need to have a thousand different ingredients in your kitchen? No, but it does mean that in addition to the bread, pasta, crackers, and cake (all wheat-based), stock some potatoes and rice for your starch quota. If you're buying canned or frozen veggies, buy something other than peas. If hot cereal is a popular item, select several different kinds, so that you're getting a variety of nutrients. (Store your cereal in airtight containers or food bags so they don't go stale.) Experiment with various textures and flavors of tofu or seitan. If you'll be using your microwave to heat up frozen vegan entrées or side dishes, keep a wide selection to choose from so you're not eating the same food for dinner every night.

More Food for Thought

1. Beans! Beans! We have found canned kidney, black, white, limas, butter (baby limas), garbanzo, soybean, and lentils, to name a few. Yes, fresh or frozen beans are generally higher in nutrients and lower in sodium than canned beans, but canned beans are better than no beans and are good add-in ingredients. Canned beans take less cooking time, too.

2. We like to keep canned corn, green beans, wax beans, sliced or julienne beets, sliced carrots, sauerkraut, pickled red cabbage, sliced or whole mushrooms, chopped tomatoes, whole potatoes, and mustard and collard greens on hand. On the sweet side, fruit canned in juice such as pears, plums, mandarin oranges, peaches, apricots, and cherries

are great additions to meals. Unsweetened applesauce and crushed pineapple can be used in microwave baking and in sauce preparation.

3. Dried items are handy, too. Dried dates, apricots, figs, raisins, prunes, apples, peaches, nectarines, cranberries, cherries, and blueberries are just some of the dried fruit that you can toss into microwaved foods. Dried fruit is high in (natural) sugar, but as far as snacks and ingredients go, they are chock-full of nutrients. Sundried red and yellow tomatoes, dried veggie soup mixes, dried mushrooms, and dried chilies are easy additions to soups, salads, pastas, and combination dishes.

4. Think ethnic. Just picture it: you unceremoniously dump a can of white beans into a bowl. Big deal. Now you toss in some salsa. Hmmm, getting better. For you fire-eaters out there, add some pickled jalapeños and hot sauce. Throw your feast into the microwave and heat until it's hot and you've got something great! Prowl Indian stores for curry pastes and powders, aromatic sauce mixes, tandoori rubs (great for vegetables and tofu), pickled veggies, chutneys, long-grained rice, and interesting breads and cracker breads. Visit Middle Eastern stores for spices, hummus and tahini, harira (a fiery chili paste), pomegranate molasses (makes a wonderful addition to salad dressings and cold beverages), nut and seed blends, and breads. Asian markets yield different varieties of tofu, soy beverages, spices, sauces, great canned fruits and vegetables, long- and short-grained rice, and different varieties of produce.

5. Here's some quick pasta tips: fresh pasta sold in the refrigerated section of the market can be frozen, so you don't have to eat that entire package of angel hair pasta at one time. Cook what you'll eat and freeze the rest (remember to label!). Pasta comes in other colors besides white. Try spinach, carrot, tomato, mushroom, chili, and lemon-basil, to name a few. All dried pasta can be prepared in the microwave, although fresh pasta cooks quicker. Cooked pasta tossed with sauce and veggies makes a fast microwave casserole. (Note: Make sure the fresh pasta is vegan and does not contain eggs.)

6. Oil'll be darned. While watching the fats on the menu, oil is still an important ingredient, adding flavor and color. Olive oil is flavorful and monounsaturated (one of the good guys). Sesame seed and hazelnut oils are specialty oils that give unique flavors to dishes. If you're selecting just plain vegetable oils, read the label to find the least unsaturated kind. Vegetable oil sprays are very useful for cooking. Margarines are not necessarily vegan (or unsaturated), so read the labels for the healthiest type. Some health experts advise limiting the amount of trans-fatty acids in the diet. These can be found in solid margarines and products such as cookies or snack bars made with solid margarines. Again, read the label. You'll want to really limit products that contain palm, tropical, and coconut oils, since they are saturated fats. Just remember, 2 teaspoons of most oils are about 50 calories, all from fat (just for perspective, about 4 ounces of fruit juice is about 60 calories with no fat, and a half-cup of most cooked veggies is 25 calories with no fat).

7. Nuts, seeds, and nut butters add flavor and interest to your meals. Oatmeal can become exciting with some walnut or pecan crunch and soups can be garnished with toasted almonds or sesame seeds. We've seen soy, hazelnut, cashew, and almond butter on the market shelf. They are tasty, but high in fat; used sparingly, they can add a lot of flavor, color, and crunch to the menu.

8. Mix and match. For example, a can of tomato soup. Yawn. But how about a can of tomato soup with some canned mushrooms added.... and some smoky seitan.... and some canned garbanzo beans.... and some leftover baked potato. Microwave and savor! Add nuts and dried fruit, frozen and fresh berries to muffin mixes, canned mushrooms and dried chilies to that cup-a-noodles, or some granola and nuts into that hot cereal.

9. Think ethnic, revisited. When you go to a restaurant in an ethnic area, check out the neighborhood groceries. You'll probably find some vegan convenience ingredients that will spice up your meals. Indulge in frozen entrées and side dishes, or soup, sauce, or dessert mixes. Indian dahl (lentil soup, used as a universal condiment), Mexican tamales (many places are making them with vegetable oil instead of lard, just ask), Persian pita, Israeli falafel, Thai mango and sticky rice, and Russian beet borscht are just some of the prepared items we like to bring home and microwave on demand. You can base a wonderful meal around any of these.

10. Spice rack. Always keep handy both sweet staples (cinnamon, nutmeg, orange zest, ground ginger, cloves, etc.) and the savory (granulated garlic, black and white pepper, onion powder, dried basil, oregano, thyme, red pepper

flakes, curry powder, dried parsley, etc.). Add spice blends such as lemon-pepper or Cajun spices, if you know you'll use them. Discard dried herbs and spices that have lost their zing. Even if stored in a cool, dry place in an airtight container, most dried herbs and spices lose their flavoring capacity after a year.

11. Look in the refrigerator. Depending upon your preferences, have a nice stock of firm and silken tofu, tempeh, and/or seitan. Purchase these plain or flavored. Fake meats, such as deli slices, tofu dogs, and breakfast crumbles freeze well and are great add-in ingredients. Tofu, tempeh, and seitan also freeze well. For example, if you take a package of tofu and a package of soy crumbles out of the freezer in the morning and leave them in the refrigerator, they'll be thawed by the time you are ready to make dinner. Mix the crumbles with some chopped veggies, whisk in the tofu, top with salsa or tomato sauce, and microwave and you'll have a fast, hot meal.

12. Say cheese — soy cheese, that is. There are lots of vegan cheese and alternative "dairy" products on the market today, such as flavored, shredded, and sliced soy cheese, soy sour cream, and soy yogurt. Experiment with the brands and the products until you find the ones you like. Most soy cheese can be frozen.

13. Bread and crackers are even faster to use than pasta or rice and some freeze very well. You can make a quick microwave "pizza" if you've got English muffins or bagels in the freezer and chopped tomatoes and tomato sauce in the pantry. Quick burritos require tortillas.

14. Rooting for the veggies. Root vegetables can be stored for a long time, so select your favorites from white potatoes, purple potatoes (called Peruvian purples, they are dark purple on the outside and lavender on the inside), Yukon golds, sweet potatoes, carrots, onions, garlic, beets, and turnips. Give them a dark, cool home and steam them in the microwave when ready. Top a white baked potato with canned lentils and salsa, or a sweet potato with crushed pineapple, mashed tofu, dried cranberries, and canned mandarin oranges.

We realize these ideas sound like a lot of food to have on hand, and it is. You need to select the items you like and will use. Remember that you have to decide on the balance between a nicely stocked kitchen and over-the-top. Make your kitchen a friendly, welcoming place. Know that when you are thinking about what to have for breakfast, what to pack for lunch, or what to make for dinner, there are lots of ingredients you can enjoy and combine to make healthy, pleasing meals. Your time in the kitchen, and your meal times for sure, should be pleasant, encouraging times. Your microwave will save you time, and, if you plan carefully, some clean-up.

Overall Kitchen Safety

You might not want to add a story about *E.coli* or *Salmonella* inundating your home to your colorful party repertoire, so clean well. Just because you don't have animal products around, doesn't mean there aren't any food-borne illness-causing bacteria lurking. Bacteria like protein, whether it's from meat or from beans, rice, pasta, soy products, etc. Bacteria don't grow well below 40 degrees or above 140 degrees, so keep food either hot or cold, but not in-between.

Keep lots of towels, soap, bleach, or bleach alternatives on hand. If you use sponges and towels, sanitize them frequently with diluted bleach or in the dishwasher. Bacteria are rendered harmless by water that is over 180 degrees or by chlorine, so make your choice (you don't need both, just one or the other). If you have a dishwasher, use it! In addition to dishes, you can run kitchen sponges, small soap dishes or containers, and vegetable scrubbers through the dishwasher.

Use clean containers to store your foods. Every container should have a lid or be covered with tight-fitting plastic wrap. Never store food in aluminum foil or in opened, original cans. If you open a can of peaches, store the leftover peaches in a covered bowl or cup, not the can.

Avoid cross contamination. Wash and sanitize knives, cutting boards, containers, and your hands when preparing different ingredients or dishes. Wipe down your microwave with a sanitizing cloth between uses. This prevents the ingredients from one food from mixing with the ingredients from another; in turn, this helps to keep down the bacterial count.

Okay, now you're stocked and ready. Let's plan some meals.

CHAPTER TWO
Vegan Menu Planning

Introduction

Microwave cooking saves on time and the number of dishes and utensils needed to prepare a menu item. As a result, it will be easier to have greater variety in your meals.

Everyone should think about what he or she will eat throughout the day. Each meal does not need to be balanced, but the total day needs to include a wide variety of food. Try to eat at least 1 serving of fruits and vegetables at each meal, totaling at least 6 servings per day. When you can, select whole grains rather than highly processed grain products. Whole wheat or vegetable pasta (such as carrot or spinach), brown rice, and wheat berry bread offer more nutrition than white flour pasta, white rice, and white bread. Fat and salt don't add a lot to the health profile of your diet. Experiment with healthy ingredients that are just as acceptable as salt and fat, in terms of taste and texture. For example, a squeeze of lemon or some chopped basil will perk up a pasta sauce just as well as a sprinkle of salt. Applesauce and fruit purées add texture to baked goods without the fat.

Become a label reader, if you are not already. Hidden salt can appear as soy sauce, MSG, and sea salt on the label. Fat is a little more difficult to hide: look for vegetable oil and margarine. To find out information about food ingredients, you may want to go to <www.vrg.org>.

Vegan diets are generally lower in saturated fat than non-vegetarian diets. Saturated fat in the vegan diet comes from coconut oil, palm oil, and other tropical oils. These foods should be limited. Vegan diets do not contain cholesterol. However, vegan diets can be high in fat. If you use a lot of margarine or oil in cooking, order fried foods when dining out, or eat a lot of processed snack foods, such as potato chips, you are adding a lot of fat to your diet. Try to be moderate in your use of fat-containing ingredients.

Both polyunsaturated fats and monounsaturated fats are more healthful than saturated fats. Foods that are high in these better fats include olives, avocado, vegetable oils (like canola oil and olive oil), nuts, and seeds. Remember that according to the US Dietary Guidelines, your daily calories from fat should be less than 30% of total calories. Some groups recommend that you get no more than 20% of your calories from fat. So if you eat about 2,000 calories, you have about 600 fat calories to play around with. To give you some reference, the following contain about 50 calories of fat: 1-1/3 teaspoons of vegetable oil (any type, because oil is oil when it comes to calories), about 10 large ripe olives, 2 teaspoons solid margarine, and 1/8 of an avocado.

Some people speak about "vegan nutrition issues." They are usually referring to the amount of protein, iron, calcium, and vitamin B12 found in the vegan diet. Actually, these nutrients should be of concern to everyone. Of course, if you maintain a well-balanced diet every day, it isn't difficult to obtain particular nutrients. If you're eating a varied diet with lots of fruits and veggies, soy products, beans, and the other good stuff you've read about, you should be doing okay!

Consuming adequate protein is easy. If you eat a varied whole foods diet with the proper amount of calories, you'll probably take in enough protein. Until several years ago, protein planning or protein combining was thought to be essential for vegetarians. It was believed that you conscientiously had to eat specific combinations of plant foods at every meal, such as rice and beans or lentils and pasta, in order to guarantee the intake of complete proteins. In reality, both animal and plant proteins contain all the essential amino acids but plant proteins often contain lower amounts of some essential amino acids than do animal proteins. We now know that by eating a variety of plant foods over the course of the day, you'll have the proper protein intake. Live not just on apples and broccoli; throw in some soymilk, hummus, or a bean burrito, too. (By the way, soy products are a good source of high quality protein.) If you have days when you know that you're just not going to be able to eat a variety of protein foods (like beans, whole grains, and nuts), try to include some soymilk, edamame (look it up in this book's Glossary!), tofu, or a soy burger.

Iron and vitamin C make a great team. When you eat iron- and vitamin C-containing foods, your body is able to absorb more iron than if you just ate the iron-rich food alone. Vitamin C-containing foods include oranges, grapefruits, tangerines, kiwi fruit, strawberries, tomatoes, peppers and chilies, mangos and papayas, and green veggies like broccoli and kale. Some iron-rich foods include lentils, black-eyed peas, soybeans, bok choy, dried apricots, all kinds of greens (mustard, kale, beet, chard, spinach, etc.), blackstrap molasses, black beans, garbanzo beans, seitan, tempeh, and iron-enriched cereals and grain products. With this variety, you'll be set!

Many iron-rich foods are also good sources of calcium. Foods that provide both calcium and iron include greens and green vegetables (such as broccoli and okra), blackstrap molasses, and calcium-set tofu*. Some vegan milks are fortified with calcium, so select brands that offer this bonus. Nuts and seeds can be a modest source of calcium (for perspective, 1/2 cup of firm tofu has about 200 milligrams of calcium and 1/4 cup of almonds has about 90 milli-grams). Sneak in calcium wherever you can. Use a fortified soymilk for your morning cereal, add tofu* to your salad dressing, and toss some chopped almonds and sesame seeds in your salad.

Vitamin B12 is an important vitamin for nerve and red blood cell health. The daily requirement is very low and vegans can obtain vitamin B12 from fortified products such as cold cereal and vegan milks. Be sure to read the labels! Nutritional yeast (see the glossary for more details) may be fortified with vitamin B12. Red Star Company has a nutri-tional yeast product formulated for vegans called Vegetar-ian Support Formula™. Nutritional yeast has a cheese-like, malty flavor and can be sprinkled on cereal, blended into smoothies, and added to baking recipes, salad dressings, soups, and stir-fries.

*Read labels on tofu and select brands that contain at least 10% of the Daily Value (DV) for calcium in a serving.

Basic Information for Daily Vegan Meal Planning
(adapted from *Meatless Meals for Working People*, Wasserman and Stahler, 2001)

1. High-Protein Foods (5 servings/day)

1/2 cup tofu   1/2 cup cooked beans or legumes
1/2 cup tempeh   1 cup fortified soymilk   1/4 cup nuts
1/4 cup peanuts   2 Tablespoons peanut, nut, or soy butter
1-1/2 ounces fake meats or meat analogs

2. Grains and Whole Grains (6-10 servings per day)

1 slice whole grain, whole wheat, or rye bread
1 whole wheat waffle or pancake
2x2-inch serving of corn bread
2 Tablespoons wheat germ or wheat or oat bran
1/4 cup sunflower, sesame, or pumpkin seeds
1 ounce whole grain cereal, such as bran flakes or whole
  wheat Cherrios
1/2 cup whole grain cooked cereal, such as oatmeal
1/2 cup cooked grains, such as brown rice, barley, bulgur,
  amaranth, quinoa, or kasha
1/2 cup cooked whole grain or vegetable pasta

3. Veggies (4-6 servings per day)

• At least 2 of the following per day (1/2 cup cooked or 1 cup raw): broccoli, broccoflower, brocollini (a cross between chard and Chinese broccoli), Chinese flowering broccoli, broccoli rabe, Brussels sprouts, green cabbage, Napa cabbage, endive, chicory, kale, Swiss chard, mustard, collard or beet greens, spinach, Romaine lettuce, carrots, sweet potatoes, winter squash (such as butternut or spaghetti squash), tomatoes, bell peppers

• An additional 2 or more servings of the above veggies or any other veggies

4. Fruit (2-3 servings per day)

• At least 2 servings of the following per day: cantaloupe or other orange-fleshed melons, watermelon, mango, papaya, orange, grapefruit, tangerine, peach, apricot, kiwi fruit, strawberries, or vitamin C-enriched juices

• At least 1 additional serving of fresh, dried, or canned (in water or juice) fruit

5. At least 2 servings of fats, especially fats high in omega-3 fatty acids like flaxseed, canola, or soy oil. A single serving equals 1 teaspoon.

Be sure to include good sources of calcium (at least 8 servings per day), which include fortified soy products, almonds, fortified fruit juice, greens such as kale, turnip and collard greens, and calcium-set tofu; and reliable sources of vitamin B12, which include fortified cereals, fortified nutritional yeast products, fortified soymilks, and fortified fake meats.

Sample Menu
* items = microwaveable foods

Breakfast
Orange juice or pink grapefruit sections

Corn muffin* with peanut butter and fruit preserves or whole grain hot cereal* with soymilk

Sliced banana or cantaloupe chunks

Lunch
Lentil soup* or hummus and crackers

Pita sandwich with steamed veggies* or pasta salad with veggies and olives

Carrot salad with vegan mayonnaise or baked sweet potato* with vegan margarine

Fresh pear or apple

Dinner
Tomato bisque* or sliced kiwi and strawberries

Baked vegetable lasagna* or baked eggplant and mushrooms*

Dinner roll or breadsticks with vegan margarine

Tossed green salad with vinaigrette or carrot sticks and radishes

Apple cobbler* or soy ice cream with dried fruit

<u>Snacks</u>

Graham crackers with peanut or hazelnut butter and
fortified soymilk

Popcorn* sprinkled with Red Star Vegetarian Support
Formula™ (nutritional yeast) and orange-cranberry juice

Soymilk, banana, and fruit smoothie

Warm bagel with fruit preserves or apple butter*

Microwave Meal Planning

Just as with any type of cooking, when you think about
microwave cooking, think about how many healthy ingredients you can "sneak" into the preparation. Use the
planning guide we've provided in conjunction with your
creativity to make the healthiest foods possible. Here are
some ideas:

- Make canned soups "creamy" by stirring in some silken
tofu or soymilk.
- Chop leftover cooked vegetables or thawed frozen vegetables and add them to canned soups for extra vitamins,
minerals, and fiber.
- Use vegan milks as part of the liquid for preparing microwaved hot cereals.
- Add leftover cooked beans or lentils or canned or fresh
sliced mushrooms to canned soups.
- Purée leftover beans or cooked vegetables and stir them
into tomato or mushroom sauce.
- Use vegetable broths or vegetable juices to replace some of
the cooking liquid for soups and sauces.
- Stir a dab of peanut butter or other nut butter into hot
cereals or hot cocoa before you microwave. This adds a
small amount of protein and some vitamins and minerals.

- Add chopped dried fruit or nuts to hot cereal prior to microwaving.
- Use applesauce or fruit purées to replace some of the fat in microwave baking recipes.
- Don't serve pasta plain. Toss pasta with chopped tomatoes, bell peppers, onions, salsa, or your favorite mixed vegetable combination, or add chopped firm tofu prior to microwaving.
- Have chopped nuts, wheat germ, and nutritional yeast handy to sprinkle on foods as a garnish.

You get the idea. Remember that microwaving will save the natural moisture in most foods and bring out the flavor. Extra ingredients will add to the nutrient content as well as the flavor and texture of your microwaved foods.

Microwave Creativity
You're bound to have leftovers of conventionally prepared and microwaved foods. Use these items to prepare new meals — chefs do this all the time.

For example, tomato shortcake, a savory entrée popularized by Executive Chef David Turk of Indiana Market and Catering, is made by layering polenta or cornbread with salsa, chopped olives, and fresh basil, and garnished with vegan sour cream. This dish can be microwaved to keep it tender and steamy. That's just one of the things you can do with that extra pan of cornbread you decided to make. Here are some more ideas for combining leftovers to create nutritious meals:

Chili Rice: combine leftover cooked rice with leftover cooked beans, canned tomatoes, a little garlic, a little onion, and chili powder, and microwave until bubbly.

Shepherd's Pie: combine leftover soy crumbles with leftover tomato soup or sauce, and frozen peas and carrots; top all with leftover mashed potatoes, and microwave until heated thoroughly.

Taco Pasta: layer leftover taco "meat" with leftover pasta, frozen spinach, shredded vegan cheese, and salsa. Microwave until heated thoroughly.

Mushroom Stuffing: add cooked or canned chopped mushrooms to boxed vegan stuffing mix. You can microwave this on its own for a side dish, or use it to stuff tomatoes, bell peppers, onions, or summer squash.

Corn Chowder: combine cooked corn, chopped canned tomatoes, diced canned or cooked potatoes, silken tofu, and tomato juice. Mix to combine and microwave until bubbly.

Tofu-Veggie Stew: combine your favorite canned vegetable soup with vegetable broth, leftover cooked veggies, and small chunks of extra firm tofu. Mix to combine and microwave until bubbly.

Fruit Crumble: chop and mix leftover canned fruit with a small amount of applesauce. Top with granola, crumbled cake crumbs, and chopped fruit, and microwave until bubbly.

Sweet Patootie: mash cooked sweet potatoes with crushed pineapple, orange juice concentrate, powdered ginger, maple syrup, and cinnamon. Top with additional crushed pineapple. Microwave until heated through. Use as a side dish with savory entrées or as a hot dessert with a small scoop of sorbet.

<u>Hot and Fruity Applesauce</u>: mix leftover applesauce with a small amount of raisins and some finely diced canned fruit, such as peaches or pineapples. Heat until bubbly. You can add this to your hot cereal in the morning, eat it as a hot and quick snack, spoon it over sorbet or vegan frozen dessert, or serve it with a savory entrée.

More Ideas for Vegan Microwave Meals

<u>Breakfast</u>
- Hot oatmeal or hot cereal microwaved with chopped walnuts, dried apricots, and canned or fresh peaches.

- Hot Smoothie: microwave mocha cappuchino made with instant coffee, almond milk, cocoa powder, and puréed banana.

- Hot Fruit for Breakfast: microwave canned or fresh peaches and pears combined with dried apricots and raisins, cinnamon, ginger, and a small amount of apple juice.

- Breakfast Rice Pudding: combine leftover rice mixed with rice milk or vanilla soymilk, cinnamon, raisins, and chopped nuts, then microwave.

- Old Fashioned Cornmeal Mush: crumble leftover corn-bread into a bowl covered with soymilk; microwave until hot. Some people like to make this sweet by adding maple syrup and others enjoy adding vegan margarine and vegan cheese.

Packing a lunch (If you have a microwave at the office or school, you can heat up your meal.)

- Pack a leftover baked potato, along with containers of soy sour cream and salsa.

- Pack a leftover baked sweet potato along with containers of mashed firm tofu and crushed pineapple.

- Pack some leftover beans, tortillas, vegan cheese, and some shredded lettuce to assemble a burrito or a burrito salad; do the same thing with pita or flatbread.

- Pack leftover vegan ravioli along with a container of tomato soup. When you combine the two, you'll have ravioli soup!

- Pack an English muffin or a bagel, along with a container of tomato sauce, some shredded vegan cheese, sliced olives, and canned mushrooms (you can make little packets of plastic wrap to cut down on the number of containers); assemble a microwave pizza at lunchtime.

- For dessert, pack a baking apple you have cored and dipped in some lemon or orange juice (to prevent browning), along with a packet of maple syrup and a packet of combined cinnamon, ginger, and nutmeg. Pour the syrup over the apple and sprinkle on the spices. Microwave until the apple is soft.

Dinner

- Prepare a cold salad, put some soup in the microwave, and enjoy! While you're eating the soup, have a pasta or bean casserole (leftover) warming in the microwave; prepare some rice in the microwave and set aside.

- Assemble a bean chili or a lentil stew and microwave. Serve the chili or stew over the rice; microwave a baked potato and set aside.

- Select your favorite sauce and pour it over a portion of extra firm tofu. While the tofu is microwaving, dress up your baked potato with chopped veggies, salsa, vegan sour cream, vegan shredded cheese, and so on. Take the tofu out of the microwave and pop the potato back in for just 1 minute of heating before chowing down.

- Layer leftover cornbread with mashed cooked beans, salsa, and cooked veggies. Pour some plain tomato sauce over the cornbread and microwave until hot. While the cornbread is microwaving, prepare some veggie sticks and some hummus.

(Note: Many of the techniques to prepare the items above are found in later chapters.)

CHAPTER THREE
Converting Traditional Recipes to the Microwave

Introduction

Knowing how to convert recipes from traditional cooking to microwave cooking can help you when you want to free up your oven and range top during large meal preparation. Microwaving also comes in handy during the summer, when you may not want to turn on the stove and warm up the kitchen. Many recipes can be converted from traditional cooking methods to microwave cooking methods. In this chapter we'll explain how to approach the recipes you've prepared on a range top or in an oven and transfer them into microwaveable dishes.

We've only discussed recipes that use an uncomplicated microwave, that is, one without a browning unit or broiling unit. This means that we haven't included many baking recipes. If your microwave has a browning unit, you may want to do some exploring on your own. Just follow the basic guidelines we've provided you.

When converting recipes, choose familiar ones. You'll want to be very comfortable preparing recipes traditionally before you convert them to microwave cooking.

How to Select Recipes to Convert

Choose recipes that you've prepared several times. If you know how a recipe is supposed to look and taste at various stages of preparation, you'll find it easier to tell if you are on the right track when using a microwave. Moist foods work very well in a microwave, so think of soups, sauces, vegetables, cereals, hot beverages, rice, pasta, and tofu dishes to start.

Foods that require browning or deep-frying do not work well in a microwave. (Piecrusts can be done in a microwave, but they take patience and skill.) Foods that are supposed to end up crispy, dry, or with a crust will not be a great success in the microwave.

You can use the microwave to assist with recipes that will not be finished in a microwave. For example, you don't want to do stir-fries in a microwave, but you can defrost the vegetables, make a sweet and sour sauce, and prepare rice to serve with the stir-fry in the microwave.

Selecting Microwave Cooking from Conventional Methods

Traditional recipes will call for different cooking techniques. The following is a quick "translation" from traditional to microwave methods for you to use:

Traditional	Microwave
Roasting	Microwave Roasting: food is elevated on a rack, not covered, usually cooked at MEDIUM (50%)
Stewing	Microwave Stewing or Braising: ingredients can't be browned, liquids will be reduced; usually cooked at MEDIUM (50%) in a covered casserole or cooking bag
Poaching	Microwave Poaching: liquid is reduced to less than 1 cup to produce steam; the dish will be covered with vented plastic wrap or a fitted lid
Steaming	Microwave Steaming: moist ingredients can be cooked in a microwave in a tightly covered dish with no water
Sautéing or Stir-fry	Sautéing or Stir-frying: Can't be done in a microwave (no browning and crispness), unless your microwave has a browning unit
Baking	Microwave Baking: some moist quick breads, such as cornbread, muffins, or carrot cake, can be baked in the microwave (see details that follow)

Estimating Time and Testing for Doneness

The difference between microwave and conventional cooking is cooking time. Microwave ovens differ in speed and evenness of cooking. Some work well when loaded with food and some work better with less. You'll have to build a working relationship with your microwave so that you can have the best culinary success.

The first time you prepare a microwave recipe, you'll want to watch carefully to get a feel for time, the need to rotate the cooking dish, or to stop the cooking process and stir. You may need to add a little more liquid than has been called for in the recipe or reduce the cooking time.

Most important, you'll want to test and taste. You can test for doneness by looking (is the sauce bubbly?), by feeling (remove a piece of carrot and see if it snaps or bends in your hand), and by tasting (does the potato flake in your mouth?). Tasting helps to assess doneness and the need to adjust seasonings.

In terms of time, most microwave experts will tell you that microwave cooking generally should take 25-50% less time than conventional cooking. This is just a generalization or a starting point. It will depend on the amount of food you're placing in the microwave, the desired degree of doneness, and the microwave's power.

Ingredient Tips

There are some tricks of the trade when it comes to ingredient usage for converting from conventional to microwave recipes. We'll let you in on our secrets.

1. You'll find that microwaving concentrates flavors, reducing the need for salt. Try reducing the salt called for in the recipe by half. You can always add more salt while cooking or before serving the dish.

2. Use quicker cooking rice and grains. Although you certainly can prepare unpolished brown rice or basmati rice in the microwave, you may find that you'd like to save some time, since that's what using a microwave is all about. You can find quick-cooking versions of many types of your favorite rice, barley, and couscous (note that couscous is not actually a grain, but a pasta made from semolina flour).

3. If a recipe must be browned, than preheat your conventional oven and plan on allowing the microwaved dish to brown in the oven for 10-20 minutes, depending on the recipe. You may have to transfer cooking containers if the container you use is not dual-purposed for both microwave and conventional ovens. For example, if you would like a 2-quart potato casserole to brown, microwave it in a glass casserole and transfer it to a 400-degree oven to finish baking, uncovered, for 10 minutes. If you have a browning unit in your microwave, read the directions for converting times from traditional to microwave cooking.

4. If cooking pasta from a raw state, use the full amount of liquid called for on the box or in the recipe. Cover very tightly to create steam. Start on HIGH and halfway through the cooking process (about 1 minute after the water has boiled), lower to MEDIUM. This gives the pasta time to soften.

5. If microwaving vegan milk, watch it, so it doesn't boil over or form a skin. If it does form a skin, stir the skin until it dissolves (you have to do this while the milk is still hot) and use the milk right away.

6. Soymilk has a tendency to curdle when added to hot liquids. This can be remedied in two ways. You can whip the soymilk vigorously while adding it to a hot liquid or

heat the soymilk so it is the same temperature as the liquid to which it will be added.

7. When cooking vegetables, especially in soups or sauces, you'll want to dice them finely. Sliced or coarsely chopped vegetables take longer to cook and may not cook evenly.

8. Tofu contains a lot of liquid and may fall apart when microwaved. If you would like your final product to have cubes or strips of tofu, than you can purchase extra firm tofu. You can use extra firm tofu for microwaving when the traditional recipe calls for firm. Or you can firm up your tofu by removing it from the package, placing it in a non-metallic strainer and weighing it down with several dinner plates. You can place this in the refrigerator and let it drain for several hours (or over-night). This will remove some of the tofu's moisture and give you a firmer product.

9. You will probably be cutting back on oil or fat in micro-wave recipes. Since ingredients usually don't stick in the microwave, less fat can be used to produce a satisfactory product.

Baking in the Microwave

Remember that items baked in a microwave don't brown, so select whole grain or dark-colored recipes, such as whole wheat bread or carrot cake.

Yeast dough for microwaving needs extra shortening to prevent dryness or a tough crust. If you are trying out some of your conventional baking recipes in the microwave, a good rule of thumb for microwaving is about 1/4 cup shortening, such as vegan margarine or vegetable fat, for every 3 cups of flour.

Even if you aren't going to bake bread in your micro-wave, you can use the microwave as a proofer. You can do the initial proofing by placing dough in a bowl with 1 cup of water beside it and use the LOW or 10% setting. You can tell your dough is successfully proofed when it has doubled in size. So eyeball your dough before you put in in the microwave. Try two or three minutes of microwaving and check the dough. If it has doubled in size, it's sufficiently proofed. If not, try microwaving in increments of 2 minutes until doubling is achieved.

To convert conventional baking recipes to microwave baking recipes, use the following guide:

For Muffins: add 1-2 Tablespoons more shortening for each cup of flour. Use 2 paper liners for each muffin to absorb additional moisture. Position the muffins in a ring in the microwave for even baking.

For Biscuits: microwaved biscuits do not brown. Place them in a ring and leave room for extra rising.

For Quick Breads (such as zucchini breads): chop fruit or nuts very finely. Add 2 Tablespoons more shortening.

For Coffeecakes: add 1-2 more Tablespoons shortening and reduce baking powder by one quarter.

Ingredients That Don't Work
If any of the following ingredients are necessary to the success of a recipe, than you'll want to use conventional cooking methods. Microwaves are not friendly to every ingredient. We've listed several that we've not had success with:

Puff pastry
Piecrust from scratch or double-crusted pies
Layered, uncooked potato casseroles that can't be stirred
Regular pizza dough
Deep-fried anything
Casseroles layered with bread; however, breadcrumbs
    work

Breads or rolls that require a hard crust or to be
   browned
Waffles and pancakes (need to be grilled on a hard
   surface)
Layer cakes (bake unevenly and do not brown)

How to Use This Chapter
When you are ready to convert some of your traditional
recipes to microwave recipes, look to see if any of the
following recipes are fairly similar. This will give you a
good guide for cooking time, liquid amounts, and cooking
containers.

   You get two for the price of one with the following
recipes. Each recipe is a traditional recipe with microwave
conversions. This will show you where it's necessary to
make changes. Nutritional analyses for the recipes are for
the microwave version. (Note: Traditional recipes are in
regular print and the microwave conversions are printed in
italics.)

SOUPS

Some people use their microwave to reheat prepared soups
and to save time when cooking soups from scratch. Depending on the ingredients, microwaving soups from
scratch may or may not cut down on the cooking time. For
example, vegetable soups cook very quickly, sometimes in
as little as 10 minutes. Bean soups, on the other hand, can
take up to an hour in a microwave.

   Microwaving soups from scratch is not a quick process,
but will be faster than cooking them on top of the stove.
You'll do less stirring and less worrying about sticking and
burning. Ingredients tend to keep their shape and soups
thicken more naturally. Microwaving helps retain nutrients
in soup ingredients and bring out flavors.

Conventionally cooked soups made with dried beans, peas, or legumes must be simmered for a long time, and stirred frequently to avoid sticking. Beans will rehydrate in a microwave in a short time. They require little or no stirring during cooking.

You may decide to do a combination of soup cooking, soaking beans in the microwave, and simmering on the stove. In Chapter Seven you'll find an explanation on how to soak or rehydrate soups in a microwave.

Split Pea Soup
(Makes 2 quarts or 8 cups)

2 quarts *(hot)* water
2 cups green or yellow split peas
1 cup diced onion
1/2 teaspoon dried dill
1/2 teaspoon black pepper
1/2 cup sliced *(diced)* celery
1/2 cup sliced *(diced)* carrots

In a large pot *(5-quart casserole)*, combine water, peas, onion, dill, and pepper. Cover and bring to a boil; lower heat and simmer for 1-1/2 hours, stirring occasionally. *(Cover and microwave on HIGH for 40 minutes, stirring occasionally or until peas are tender.)*

Remove lid and add celery and carrots. Cook uncovered over medium heat 40-50 minutes, or until vegetables are tender and soup is thick. *(Microwave on MEDIUM uncovered for 20 minutes or until the vegetables are tender and soup is thick.)*

Total Calories Per Cup: 183	Total Fat as % of Daily Value: 1%	
Protein: 12 gm Fat: <1 gm	Carbohydrates: 34 gm	Calcium: 36 mg
Iron: 3 mg Sodium: 37 mg	Dietary Fiber: 8 gm	

Vegetable-Corn Soup
(Makes about 2 quarts or 8 cups)

Vegetable oil spray *(omit)*
2 cups cooked or canned, drained, white beans
5 cups water or vegetable stock *(reduce amount to 4 cups, divided into 1 cup and 3 cups, to be used at different times)*
1 teaspoon black pepper
1/2 teaspoon dried thyme
1 bay leaf
2 cups chopped canned tomatoes *(not drained)*
1-1/2 cups sliced carrots *(thinly sliced carrots)*
1 pound baking potatoes (about 3 cups), peeled and cut into large cubes *(small cubes)*
1/2 cup chopped celery
1/4 cup chopped onions
1 cup frozen, thawed corn or canned corn, drained, or fresh corn, cut off the cob

Spray a large pot with oil. Sauté beans for 2 minutes. *(Omit these steps.)*

Stir in water, black pepper, thyme, and bay leaf and simmer for 15 minutes. *(Combine beans, water, black pepper, thyme, and bay leaf in 3-quart container. Cover. Microwave on HIGH for 5 minutes.)*

Add remaining ingredients and heat to boiling. Cover and simmer on low heat for 40-50 minutes or until vegetables are tender. *(Add remaining ingredients, cover, and microwave on MEDIUM for 20 minutes or until vegetables are tender.)*

Total Calories Per Serving: 142   Total Fat as % of Daily Value: 1%
Protein: 7 gm   Fat: 1 gm   Carbohydrates: 31 gm   Calcium: 65 mg
Iron: 2 mg   Sodium: 53 mg   Dietary Fiber: 8 gm

Sandwiches heat well in the microwave. Select ones that do not require frying or browning. You'll find the sandwich filling to be hot and moist and the bread tender.

Chili Cheese Dogs
(Serves 4)

4 vegan hot dogs
1 cup prepared chili beans
4 hot dog buns
2 slices vegan cheese (see note)

Preheat broiler. *(Omit.)* Boil 1 quart of water in a medium saucepan. Place hot dogs in pan and cook over medium heat until thoroughly heated. Drain. *(Omit these steps.)*

In a small saucepan, heat chili beans over medium heat until thoroughly heated, stirring about 5 minutes. *(Place chili beans in small bowl. Microwave on HIGH for 1 minute or until heated.)*

Place vegan hot dogs in buns and spoon chili over tops. Place half a slice of cheese on top of each. Arrange on a baking sheet. Place under a broiler and cook until cheese melts, about 1 minute. *(Place vegan hot dogs in bun on a plate lined with a paper towel. Microwave on HIGH for 1 minute or until hot dogs are hot. Spoon chili beans over hot dogs and top each with 1/2 slice of cheese. Microwave on HIGH for 30-40 seconds, or until cheese melts.)*

Note: We've had good results with Vegan-Rella™, Follow Your Heart's Vegan Gourmet Cheese Alternative™, and Tofutti™ brand cheeses.

Total Calories Per Serving: 274   Total Fat as % of Daily Value: 7%
Protein: 18 gm   Fat: 5 gm   Carbohydrates: 39 gm   Calcium: 51 mg
Iron: 1 mg   Sodium: 779 mg   Dietary Fiber: 6 gm

Casseroles are a perfect match for the microwave. Micro-waves allow the flavors to meld. Below, we've given you several different casseroles to try.

Mixed Beans and Macaroni Casserole
(Serves 6)

For a conventional casserole, you would cook and drain pasta and then combine it with other ingredi-ents. With a microwave casserole, you can cook the pasta at the same time you are cooking the casserole. The trick is to use equal amounts of liquid and pasta. Below is only the microwave version of this casserole.

1-1/2 cups cooked or canned, drained beans (try a
   combination such as garbanzo and kidney or
   black beans and white beans)
1 can (10-3/4 ounces) split pea or bean soup (condensed; see note)
1 cup elbow macaroni (see note)
1 cup chopped celery
1 cup canned, drained sliced water chestnuts
1/2 cup frozen, thawed green peas
1/4 cup chopped onions
1/2 cup chopped almonds or peanuts
2 teaspoons parsley flakes
1/2 cup canned, drained sliced mushrooms
1 cup water

Combine all ingredients in a medium casserole (at least a 2-quart casserole). Cover tightly. Microwave on HIGH for 8 minutes. Reduce power to MEDIUM (50%) and microwave for 12-16 minutes, or until the pasta is tender. Stir once during cooking.

Notes: If you use smaller pasta, such as small shells, you will reduce the HIGH cooking time to 3 minutes. There are several brands of vegan condensed split pea soup on the market. We've had success with Hain Celestial Foods™ and Imagine Foods™ brands.

Total Calories Per Serving Using 3/4 Cup Each Garbanzo and Kidney Beans: 267
Total Fat as % of Daily Value: 12%

Protein: 12 gm	Fat: 8 gm	Carbohydrates: 39 gm	Calcium: 85 mg
Iron: 9 mg	Sodium: 795 mg	Dietary Fiber: 10 gm	

Casserole with Uncooked Potatoes

(Serves 5)

Vegetable oil spray *(omit)*
2 cups smoked tofu or smoked seitan, crumbled or chopped into fine pieces
5 medium baking potatoes (like Russets), about 4 cups, peeled and thinly sliced
1-1/2 cups canned vegetable soup
1 cup water *(omit)*
1/2 cup thinly sliced onions

Preheat oven to 350 degrees. *(Omit.)*

Spray a skillet with vegetable oil. Add tofu or seitan and sauté for 2 minutes. *(Place tofu or seitan in a medium casserole. Microwave on HIGH for 2 minutes. Break into smaller pieces, if possible, without making into crumbs.)*

Combine tofu, potatoes, soup, and water in a baking dish. Cover and bake for 30 minutes. Stir. *(Stir potatoes and soup into tofu in same casserole as tofu was cooked in. Cover with wax paper. Microwave on HIGH for 14-16 minutes or until potatoes are tender and liquid is absorbed.)*

Continue to bake, uncovered for 50-55 minutes or until potatoes are tender and liquid is absorbed. Sprinkle onions on top of casserole and bake for 5 minutes. *(Stir. Sprinkle onions on top of casserole and microwave, uncovered, on HIGH for 2 minutes.)*

Total Calories Per Serving: 252   Total Fat as % of Daily Value: 9%
Protein: 14 gm   Fat: 6 gm   Carbohydrates: 37 gm   Calcium: 24 mg
Iron: 1 mg   Sodium: 701 mg   Dietary Fiber: 4 gm

Tri-Colored Stuffed Summer Squash

(Serves 4)

Eggplants, summer squash, onions, hard winter squash, or peppers can be stuffed and cooked in a microwave. These are casseroles with edible containers. Some ingredients, such as rice, need to be precooked, as they would be in conventional recipes. Very hard vegetables, such as hard winter squash, should be cut, deseeded, then microwaved cut side down for 2-3 minutes before stuffing to soften them.

2 medium crookneck (yellow) squash or zucchini
1/2 cup cooked brown or white rice
1/4 cup chopped red onion
1/4 cup chopped green pepper
1/4 cup frozen, thawed cut corn or canned corn, drained or fresh corn, cut off the cob
1 teaspoon dried parsley
1/4 cup chopped fresh tomato

Preheat oven to 350 degrees. *(Omit.)*

Cut squash in half, lengthwise. Scoop out pulp, leaving a half-inch shell. In a medium bowl, combine squash pulp, rice, onions, pepper, corn, and parsley.

Place squash halves in baking dish. Divide filling in quarters, and stuff each squash half with one quarter of the filling. Top with tomatoes. Cover and baked for 20-30 minutes, or until squash shells are tender. *(Cover with waxed paper and microwave on HIGH for 5-7 minutes or until shells are tender.)*

Total Calories Per Serving: 66   Total Fat as % of Daily Value: 0%
Protein: 2 gm   Fat: 0 gm   Carbohydrates: 14 gm   Calcium: 28 mg
Iron: 1 mg   Sodium: 3 mg   Dietary Fiber: 3 gm

Tomato Baked Beans
(Serves 6)

Dried beans and peas need liquid to rehydrate, so don't reduce the amount of liquid when converting from conventional to microwave cooking. The time is almost the same, too, because of the need to rehydrate and tenderize.

Microwaved beans hold their shape more than conventionally cooked beans and are firmer. If you like really soft, mushy beans, than you'll want to stay with conventional cooking methods.

This recipe is a good source of iron and zinc!

Beans:
1 pound (about 2 cups) white or Northern beans
6 cups water
1/4 cup celery leaves (cut from tops of fresh celery)
1/2 cup chopped onion
2 Tablespoons chopped fresh parsley
3 cloves garlic, minced
1 teaspoon dried thyme
1 teaspoon black pepper

Sauce:
1-1/2 cups chopped onion
2 cloves garlic, minced
1/4 cup vegan margarine
3 Tablespoons flour
1-1/2 cups hot water
3/4 cup tomato paste

In a large, heavy pot, combine beans and water. Let stand overnight. *(Place beans in a 5-quart casserole, cover with 6 cups water, and microwave on HIGH for 8 minutes or until water boils. Allow to boil for 2 minutes. Let stand for 1 hour.)*

Add remaining ingredients for beans. Simmer, covered, for 1 hour or until the beans are tender (but not mushy). Drain and save liquid. Put beans and liquid aside. *(Add remaining ingredients for beans. Cover and microwave on MEDIUM for 45 minutes or until beans are tender. Drain and save liquid.)*

Make the sauce in a 2-quart pot by sautéing the onion and garlic in margarine until tender, about 3 minutes. Blend in flour. Stir in remaining sauce ingredients. Simmer for 20 minutes, stirring often. *(To simmer in a microwave, combine onions, garlic, and margarine in a 2-quart casserole and microwave on HIGH for 4-6 minutes or until onion is tender. Stir, and continue to microwave on HIGH for 10 minutes, or until sauce is thickened.)*

Add sauce to beans in the large pot. Simmer, covered, for 1 hour or until beans are soft, stirring often. Add saved bean liquid if beans become dry during cooking. *(Add sauce to beans in casserole. Cover and microwave on HIGH for 40 minutes or until beans are soft. Add saved bean liquid if necessary.)*

Total Calories Per Serving: 387   Total Fat as % of Daily Value: 13%
Protein: 20 gm   Fat: 9 gm   Carbohydrates: 61 gm   Calcium: 225 mg
Iron: 9 mg   Sodium: 146 mg   Dietary Fiber: 14 gm

Peanut Butter Oatmeal Cookie Bars
(Makes 20)

Bar cookies adapt easily to microwaving, since they do not need to brown. They can also be iced, frosted, or topped with nut butters or fruit preserves. Even if you have a turntable, manually rotate bar cookies at least twice during microwaving to ensure even baking of this dense batter.

4 Tablespoons peanut butter
1/4 cup dry vegan sweetener
1/4 cup brown sugar
3 Tablespoons vegan margarine
2 Tablespoons soft tofu
1/2 teaspoon vanilla
1/2 cup flour
1/2 cup quick-cooking rolled oats
1/4 teaspoon baking soda
1/4 teaspoon salt
1/2 cup vegan chocolate or carob chips
2 Tablespoons peanut butter

Preheat oven to 350 degrees and lightly grease baking pan. *(Omit.)*

In a medium bowl, cream (mash together) 4 Tablespoons peanut butter, both sweeteners, shortening, tofu, and vanilla until fluffy.

Stir together flour, oats, soda, and salt and add to peanut butter mixture. Beat for 3 minutes.

Spread batter in pan. Bake for 15 to 20 minutes. *(Microwave on HIGH 3-5 minutes or until top is dry.)* Allow bars to cool.

In a small saucepan, combine chips and peanut butter, melt over low heat, stirring constantly. *(In a small bowl, combine chips and peanut butter. Microwave on MEDIUM until melted, stirring once during cooking.)*

Frost bars with mixture.

Total Calories Per Bar: 106   Total Fat as % of Daily Value: 9%
Protein: 2 gm   Fat: 6 gm   Carbohydrates: 12 gm   Calcium: 23 mg
Iron: 1 mg   Sodium: 56 mg   Dietary Fiber: 1 gm

Corn Bread
(Serves 8)

Very moist batters, such as cornbread, need to have the
liquid reduced to work in a microwave. Because of its
natural golden color, cornbread looks good when it
emerges from the microwave.

1 cup flour
1 cup yellow cornmeal
2 Tablespoons vegan dry sweetener
4 teaspoons baking powder
1/2 teaspoon salt
1 cup rice or grain milk *(2/3 cup milk)*
1/4 cup vegetable shortening *(1/2 cup shortening)*
2 Tablespoons soft tofu *(4 Tablespoons soft tofu)*
Vegetable oil spray *(omit)*

Preheat oven to 425 degrees. *(Omit.)*
    In a medium mixing bowl, combine flour, cornmeal,
sweetener, baking powder, and salt. Add milk, shortening,
and tofu. Beat until smooth, about 1 minute.
    Grease medium baking pan. *(Omit.)* Pour batter into
greased pan. Bake for 20 minutes or until knife inserted into
center comes out clean. *(Pour into ungreased pan. Microwave
on MEDIUM for 6 minutes and rotate pan. Microwave on HIGH
for 2-5 minutes or until knife inserted into center comes out
clean.)* Let stand 5 minutes before cutting.

Notes: We used all-purpose flour for this recipe. If you would like to use whole wheat or other types of flour, you'll need to experiment.

If you would like to jazz up cornbread, you can add any of the following to this recipe:

> 3/4 cup drained canned corn or thawed frozen corn
>
> 1/4 cup finely chopped pimento (canned or roasted red pepper)
>
> 1/2 cup finely chopped green onion
>
> 1/4 cup finely chopped, deseeded fresh chili (you choose the heat)

Total Calories Per Serving Using Rice Milk: 190
Total Fat as % of Daily Value: 10%
Protein: 3 gm   Fat: 7 gm   Carbohydrates: 30 gm   Calcium: 170 mg
Iron: 2 mg   Sodium: 470 mg   Dietary Fiber: 2 gm

Chocolate Fudge
(Makes about 1 pound)

When the mood strikes, fudge can be made quickly and smoothly in a microwave. This will be one of the few times that you will grease a dish to use in the microwave. Be sure to use a container that is large enough to allow extra cooking space, as you don't want it to boil over.

Vegetable oil spray
2 cups vegan dry sweetener
1 cup soy or rice milk
2 squares unsweetened vegan chocolate
1 Tablespoon light corn syrup
2 Tablespoons vegan margarine
1 teaspoon vanilla
1/2 cup chopped nuts (optional)

Grease a casserole or loaf pan with vegetable oil spray. Set aside.

In a 2-quart heavy pot, combine sweetener, milk, chocolate, and syrup, stirring constantly over medium heat until the sugar dissolves and the mixture comes to a boil. *(In a 3-quart casserole, combine sugar, milk, chocolate, and syrup. Cover. Microwave on HIGH for 5 minutes. Mix well to melt chocolate.)*

Cook over low heat for 10-15 minutes, stirring only to prevent sticking. Remove from heat and stir in margarine. *(Microwave 10 minutes, stirring once. Remove from heat and stir in margarine.)*

Cool for 10 minutes. Add vanilla. Stir constantly with a wooden spoon until fudge is thick and starts to lose its shine. Stir in nuts, if desired.

Spread quickly into greased pans. If the fudge will be eaten within several hours, you don't need to refrigerate it. If the fudge is to be stored, wrap it in waxed paper and place in the refrigerator.

Total Calories Per 1-Ounce Serving: 135   Total Fat as % of Daily Value: 5%
Protein: 0 gm   Fat: 4 gm   Carbohydrates: 27 gm   Calcium: 43 mg
Iron: 1 mg   Sodium: 34 mg   Dietary Fiber: 1 gm

Hot Cocoa
(Serves 2)

Everyone in a hurry knows how helpful a microwave can be with beverages. We've all used it to "zap" that morning cup of coffee or tea. When you have a little more time you might want to try longer-cooking hot beverages in the microwave. There's no stirring or washing pots, as you can microwave and serve from the same container.

2-1/2 Tablespoons unsweetened cocoa powder
3 Tablespoons vegan dry sweetener
1/4 cup hot water
1-3/4 cups soy, rice, or grain milk

Combine cocoa and sweetener together in a 1-quart pot *(1-quart casserole)*. Stir in water until smooth. Heat over medium heat until mixture boils, stirring constantly. Boil for 1 minute. *(Microwave on HIGH for 45 seconds to 1 minute, or until mixture rapidly boils.)*

Add milk. Heat thoroughly, stirring frequently. *(Microwave on HIGH for 2-3 minutes, or until heated thoroughly.)* Before serving, beat with a fork until frothy.

Total Calories Per Serving: 162   Total Fat as % of Daily Value: 5%
Protein: 7 gm   Fat: 4 gm   Carbohydrates: 30 gm   Calcium: 25 mg
Iron: 1 mg   Sodium: 9 mg   Dietary Fiber: 2 gm

CHAPTER FOUR
Microwave Baking and Desserts

Introduction

Many people don't think of using their microwave to bake. It is true that some items will not do well in a microwave, especially those that are supposed to be flaky, crispy, or well-browned. This means that it is best to choose items to microwave-bake that are either naturally dark in color (such as gingerbread or spice cake), that can be frosted or topped with fruit (such as cupcakes), or that are expected to be light in color (such as biscuits or bread pudding).

We have not included microwave bread baking or yeast products in this chapter. It is possible to bake bread and other leavened products in the microwave. If you are an experienced bread baker, you may want to experiment with some of your yeast-containing recipes in the microwave. Because of the variations in microwaves and the delicate balance needed in bread baking, we have decided to focus on less rigorous types of baking in this book.

Steam is an important leavener and microwaves are great places to build up steam. Liquid-containing ingredients, such as juice concentrate, tofu, vegan milk, oil, fruit purée, and vegan margarine also contribute to microwave leavening, so be sure to measure carefully.

Since microwaving cuts down on some cooking time, you can include freshly "baked" and hot desserts with your meals. For example, jazz up that slice of banana bread by sprinkling it lightly with a small amount of molasses and microwaving it until it is warm. Don't eat those canned peaches, apricots, or pears right out of the can. Place them in a small bowl and microwave them until they are hot. Combine the warm fruit with a small amount of sorbet and you've got an interesting dessert. Better yet, top that lonely slice of banana bread and molasses with warmed, canned fruit. Now you're cooking!

Ideas for Preparing Hot Desserts When You Don't Have Time to Make Them from Scratch

Hot and Sweet Tofu: drain a cube (about an 8- to 10-ounce package) of soft tofu and place it in the center of a microwave pie plate or shallow bowl. Drizzle maple or fruit syrup liberally over the tofu. Sprinkle on a Tablespoon or so of orange juice concentrate. You can add 2-3 teaspoons of powdered ginger as well. Cover and microwave on HIGH for 3 minutes or until heated thoroughly.

Apple Pie Tofu: drain a cube of soft tofu and place it in the center of a microwaveble pie plate or shallow bowl. Cover with 3/4 cup canned apple pie filling (or other flavors of pie filling). Crumble 2 graham cracker squares or 1/4 cup granola over the pie filling. Cover and microwave on HIGH for 4 minutes, or until heated through.

Pumpkin Custard: mix 1 can (8 ounces) of unsweetened pumpkin purée with 1 cup of silken tofu in a medium bowl. Flavor with 1/4 cup maple syrup, 2 teaspoons cinnamon, and 1 teaspoon nutmeg. Mix well. Microwave on HIGH for 5 minutes or until heated through. Eat the custard on its own or with your favorite gingersnaps, graham crackers, or other cookies. You can also purchase a ready-to-use graham cracker crust, pour in the pumpkin custard, and refrigerate for 1 hour for a pumpkin custard pie.

Hot Sundaes: slice 1 or 2 bananas into a small bowl and mix with 1 cup of diced, canned peaches (not drained). Microwave on HIGH for 3 minutes or until hot. Serve over frozen sorbet or other frozen dessert.

Chocolate-Covered Cherry Fudge: combine 1-1/2 cups canned cherry pie filling with 2 Tablespoons orange juice concentrate and set aside. In a large bowl, combine 2 cups chocolate or carob chips with 1/4 cup rice milk. Microwave chips on HIGH for 1 minute or until just melted. Stir to make the mixture smooth. Stir in the cherry pie filling. Spread mixture on a baking sheet and chill for at least 1 hour. You can also fill a ready-to-use pie shell or individual tart shells with this mixture.

Chocolate-Covered Granola Sundaes: place 1 cup of chocolate or carob chips in a medium bowl and microwave on HIGH for 1 minute or until just melted. Stir to make a smooth mixture. Stir in 1-1/2 cups granola and immediately serve over frozen sorbet or soy ice cream.

Microwave Baking Techniques
Remember that baking is closer to chemistry than any other type of cooking. This is especially true with microwave baking.

When measuring dry ingredients, such as flour, dry sweetener, baking powder, or baking soda, do so in a measuring cup or with measuring spoons. Be certain to level your measures, so that you're using accurate amounts.

The same goes for vegan margarine or solid fats; you have to level your measures to get consistent, accurate amounts. If a recipe calls for a dry vegan sweetener, do not substitute liquid sweeteners, such as maple syrup or molasses. It just won't work, due to the interplay of dry and moist ingredients.

Vegan margarine and oil are not interchangeable in baking recipes. We've tried to keep most recipes as lowfat as possible. When a recipe calls for oil, melted vegan margarine won't do and when you see melted vegan magarine, oil won't do. This goes back to the chemistry of baking.

When measuring liquids, such as water, applesauce, vegan milk, or oil, get down to eye level with the measure. Looking down at a measuring cup does not give you an accurate view of the amount. You've either got to get down to its level or bring it up to yours.

Baking powder is a chemical leavening agent and loses its intensity over time, or if exposed to too much heat during storage. To get the best results, make sure your baking powder is fresh. Store it away from heat and moisture.

You'll note that most of the recipes in the other chapters of this book do not include salt. Baking recipes require salt to ensure adequate leavening. Baking powder and baking soda interact with salt. If you need to eliminate salt from baking recipes, you'll have to experiment so you get the right amount of "rise." Salt substitutes cannot take the place of salt in baking recipes.

We use silken tofu to replace eggs in baking recipes. Two Tablespoons of silken tofu corresponds roughly to 1 large egg. If you are comfortable using Energ-G Egg Replacer™ (found in some natural foods stores), you can use the equivalent of one egg's worth of Egg Replacer for every 2 Tablespoons of silken tofu.

71

Here's an entertaining tip: to flame bananas, peaches, cooked fruit salads, or baked desserts, microwave about 3-6 Tablespoons of brandy or cognac in the microwave on HIGH for 15-20 seconds. Pour into a large metallic ladle, step back, and ignite the liquid in the ladle with a match. Pour over the fruit while the liquid is still ignited. It will burn out in several seconds or can be put out by covering it with a pot lid. Of course, you want to be as safe about this as possible. Do not overfill the ladle and never do this near curtains or flammable material. Make sure you've got some water or baking soda handy in case of accident.

SAUCES AND TOPPINGS

Strawberry Sauce
(Makes about 1-1/4 cups)

Serve this quick and easy sauce over baked apples, cookies, cake, fresh fruit, bananas, or sorbet.

2 teaspoons cornstarch
1-1/4 cups (10-ounce package) sweetened frozen
   strawberries, thawed and drained (save liquid)
Saved strawberry liquid (about 1/2 cup)
1 Tablespoon lemon juice

In a small bowl or 3-cup measure, combine cornstarch and strawberry liquid. Stir in strawberries. Microwave on HIGH for 2-5 minutes, until the sauce is thickened and clear. Stir at least twice during cooking. Remove from microwave, stir, and serve warm or cool.

Notes: Frozen berries or rhubarb can be used in place of strawberries. To thaw frozen berries, place package on a plate. DO NOT do this with packages that contain metal or foil. If in a plastic bag, pierce in several places. Microwave on HIGH for 1-3 minutes or until just thawed. Do not over thaw, as there will be residual heat that will continue to thaw fruit.

Total Calories Per 1/4 Cup Serving: 55   Total Fat as % of Daily Value: 0%
Protein: <1 gm   Fat: <1 gm   Carbohydrates: 15 gm   Calcium: 7 mg
Iron: <1 mg   Sodium: 1 mg   Dietary Fiber: 1 gm

Peanut Butter-Fudge Sauce
(Makes about 1 cup)

Dip banana slices, grapes, melon cubes, or graham crackers in this quick and easy sauce or serve over fruit salad or sorbet.

1 cup vegan chocolate or carob chips
1/4 cup soy or rice milk
1/2 cup peanut butter

Place ingredients in a small bowl or glass or plastic measure that hold 2 cups. Microwave on MEDIUM for 2-4 minutes or until chips just begin to melt. Stir with a wooden spoon or rubber spatula (do not use metal) until well blended. If you would like a thinner sauce, you can add more milk.

Note: You can use other nut butters to replace the peanut butter.

Total Calories Per 1/8 Cup Serving: 211   Total Fat as % of Daily Value: 23%
Protein: 6 gm   Fat: 15 gm   Carbohydrates: 16 gm   Calcium: 73 mg
Iron: 1 mg   Sodium: 64 mg   Dietary Fiber: 2 gm

Orange Sauce
(Makes about 1-1/3 cups or 5 servings)

Serve over fruit salad, muffins, or sorbet, or mix with granola. You can also make rice into a sweet dessert by tossing it with diced fruit and this sauce.

1/2 cup vegan dry sweetener
2 Tablespoons cornstarch
1 cup boiling water
2 Tablespoons vegan margarine
2 Tablespoons fresh orange zest
1/4 cup orange juice
2 Tablespoons lemon juice

In a small bowl or glass or plastic measure that holds 3 cups, combine sweetener, cornstarch, and water. Stir in margarine. Microwave 2-4 minutes on HIGH until thickened and clear, stirring at least once. Stir in zest, along with orange and lemon juices. Serve warm.

Total Calories Per Serving: 135   Total Fat as % of Daily Value: 7%
Protein: <1 gm   Fat: 5 gm   Carbohydrates: 24 gm   Calcium: 24 mg
Iron: <1 mg   Sodium: 61 mg   Dietary Fiber: <1 gm

Crunchy Granola
(Makes 1-3/4 pounds)

This recipe could be categorized as a snack or topping—it's versatile! Stored in an airtight container, it will last for 2 weeks.

1/2 cup oil
3/4 cup vegan dry sweetener

1/4 cup maple syrup
1/4 cup water
1 teaspoon ground ginger
1/4 teaspoon ground cloves
1/2 teaspoon ground cinnamon
1 Tablespoon nutritional yeast (optional)
3 cups old-fashioned oats
1 cup shelled pumpkin or sunflower seeds
1 cup wheat germ
Vegetable oil spray

Combine oil, sweetener, syrup, water, ginger, cloves, and cinnamon in a large bowl or 3-quart casserole. Microwave on HIGH for 5-8 minutes or until slightly thickened. Stir at least twice. Add remaining ingredients. Microwave on MEDIUM for 8-10 minutes, or until golden brown, stirring every 2 minutes.

Spray baking sheet with oil. While still warm, spread granola on oiled sheet, pressing down with a spatula. Let stand until firm, about 5-10 minutes. Break into small pieces and store in an airtight container in a cool, dry place.

Note: You may add 1 cup chopped raisins, dates, cranberries, apricots, or other dried fruit right after microwaving and before spreading on baking sheet.

Total Calories Per 1 Ounce Serving: 130   Total Fat as % of Daily Value: 11%
Protein: 3 gm   Fat: 7 gm   Carbohydrates: 16 gm   Calcium: 17 mg
Iron: 2 mg   Sodium: 3 mg   Dietary Fiber: 1 gm

Gingerbread

(Makes 8x8x2-inch pan, approximately 12 servings)

Warm and spicy, serve this as a dessert or a morning treat.

1/2 cup vegan margarine
1/2 cup brewed espresso or strong coffee
4 Tablespoons silken tofu
1/2 cup vegan dry sweetener
1/2 cup molasses
1-1/2 cups all purpose flour
2 teaspoons baking powder
2 teaspoons ground ginger

Place margarine and coffee in a small bowl and microwave on HIGH for 30 seconds or until margarine is melted.

In a large bowl, beat tofu and sweetener together. Add molasses, then add coffee mixture.

Sift together flour, baking powder, and ginger. Mix into liquid and stir well to combine. Add to an 8x8x2-inch microwaveable baking dish or square casserole. Microwave on HIGH for 8 minutes or until a toothpick inserted in the center comes out clean.

Total Calories Per Serving: 197   Total Fat as % of Daily Value: 12%
Protein: 2 gm   Fat: 8 gm   Carbohydrates: 30 gm   Calcium: 87 mg
Iron: 1 mg   Sodium: 180 mg   Dietary Fiber: <1 gm

Fruit and Nut Bread
(Makes 8x8x2-inch pan, approximately 12 servings)

Eat this bread warm or cool by itself, or spread with preserves or vegan cream cheese. Make a sandwich with sliced bananas, chopped dried fruit, and nut butter.

Vegetable oil spray
1 cup chopped dates
1/4 cup chopped raisins
3/4 cup chopped pecans or walnuts
1-1/2 teaspoons baking soda
3/4 cup hot tap water
3 Tablespoons vegan margarine, softened
4 Tablespoons silken tofu
1 teaspoon lemon zest
1/2 teaspoon vanilla extract
1 cup vegan dry sweetener
1-1/2 cups all-purpose flour, sifted

Spray an 8x8x2-inch microwaveable baking pan or square casserole with oil. Set aside.

In a large bowl, combine dates, raisins, nuts, and baking soda. Mix in water and margarine. Cover and let stand for 30 minutes. Stir in remaining ingredients until well blended. Pour into the baking pan. Microwave on HIGH for 8 minutes, or until a toothpick inserted in center comes out clean. Let stand at least 10 minutes before serving.

Total Calories Per Serving: 249   Total Fat as % of Daily Value: 13%
Protein: 3 gm   Fat: 9 gm   Carbohydrates: 43 gm   Calcium: 30 mg
Iron: 1 mg   Sodium: 199 mg   Dietary Fiber: 3 gm

Pumpkin Bread

(Makes 9x5-inch or 8x4-inch loaf pan, or about 10 slices)

Don't wait for the holidays to quick-bake this wonderful cake-like bread!

1 cup all purpose flour
3/4 cup vegan dry sweetener
1 teaspoon baking powder
1 teaspoon baking soda
1 teaspoon cinnamon
1 teaspoon ginger
1/2 teaspoon nutmeg
1/4 teaspoon cloves
1/2 cup oil
4 Tablespoons silken tofu
1/2 cup chopped walnuts, almonds, or mixed nuts
  (optional)
1 cup canned pumpkin (unsweetened)
Vegetable oil spray

In a medium-size mixing bowl, mix all ingredients (except oil spray) until well-combined.

Spray a 9x5-inch or 8x4-inch loaf pan with vegetable oil or line it with waxed paper. Spread batter evenly in the pan. Place an inverted shallow bowl or saucer in the center of the microwave or use a microwave baking rack. Place the loaf pan on the bowl or rack. Microwave on MEDIUM for 9 minutes. Rotate and microwave on HIGH for 2-5 minutes. Check for readiness with a toothpick inserted in the center.

Note: If possible, use a loaf pan with straight, rather than sloped sides for microwave baking.

Total Calories Per Serving: 250 Total Fat as % of Daily Value: 23%
Protein: 3 gm   Fat: 15 gm   Carbohydrates: 27 gm   Calcium: 59 mg
Iron: 1 mg   Sodium: 182 mg   Dietary Fiber: 2 gm

Variations:

<u>Applesauce Bread</u>: use 1 cup of sweetened applesauce to replace the pumpkin

<u>Carrot Bread</u>: use 2 cups finely grated, fresh carrots instead of the pumpkin

<u>Zucchini Bread</u>: use 1-1/2 cups finely grated, fresh, unpeeled zucchini to replace the pumpkin

Banana Bread
(Makes 8x4-inch or 9x5-inch loaf, approximately 10 slices)

Use this as a dessert, the foundation of a warm breakfast, or as sandwich bread.

1 cup whole wheat flour
1/2 cup all purpose flour
1/2 cup vegan dry sweetener
1/4 cup oil
1/4 cup soy or rice milk (you can use vanilla-
   flavored, or almond milk)
4 Tablespoons silken tofu
1 cup very ripe bananas, mashed
1 Tablespoon lemon juice
1 teaspoon baking soda
1/2 teaspoon salt
1/2 cup chopped walnuts, almonds, pecans, or
   mixed nuts (optional)

Place all the ingredients in a large mixing bowl and combine until smooth.

Line the bottom of a 8x4-inch or 9x5-inch loaf pan with waxed paper. Place an inverted saucer or microwave rack in the center of the microwave. Pour batter into loaf pan. Place pan on saucer or rack. Microwave on MEDIUM for 8 minutes. Rotate pan. Microwave on HIGH for 4-8 minutes, until no uncooked batter can be seen and cake springs back to touch. Let stand for 5 minutes before slicing.

Total Calories Per Serving Without Nuts: 201
Total Fat as % of Daily Value: 9%

Protein: 3 gm	Fat: 6 gm	Carbohydrates: 36 gm	Calcium: 76 mg
Iron: 1 mg	Sodium: 350 mg	Dietary Fiber: 2 gm	

Raisin and Orange Cake

(Makes 8x4-inch or 9x5-inch loaf, approximately 10 slices)

Make an extra loaf and freeze it for later.

1 cup raisins
1 cup water
2 Tablespoons fresh orange zest
1/2 cup vegan dry sweetener
1/3 cup vegan margarine, softened
4 Tablespoons silken tofu
2 teaspoons orange juice concentrate
2 teaspoons baking powder
1/2 teaspoon baking soda
1/2 teaspoon salt
1/4 teaspoon nutmeg
1/2 teaspoon ground ginger
1-1/3 cups all-purpose flour

In a large bowl, combine raisins and water. Microwave on HIGH for 2 minutes. Stir in zest. Allow to cool.

In a separate large bowl, combine all ingredients except flour. Mix until well blended. Add in flour and mix well. Add raisin mixture and blend well.

Place an inverted saucer or microwave rack in the center of the microwave. Line the bottom of a 8x4-inch or 9x5-inch loaf pan with waxed paper. Pour batter into loaf pan.

Microwave on MEDIUM for 9 minutes. Rotate pan. Microwave on HIGH for 3-6 minutes, or until no uncooked batter can be seen and cake springs back when touched. Allow cake to cool for 5 minutes before slicing.

Total Calories Per Serving: 201   Total Fat as % of Daily Value: 9%
Protein: 3 gm   Fat: 6 gm   Carbohydrates: 36 gm   Calcium: 76 mg
Iron: 1 mg   Sodium: 350 mg   Dietary Fiber: 2 gm

Graham Cracker Molasses Bread

(Makes 8x4-inch or 9x5-inch loaf, approximately 10 slices)

Use this as a sandwich bread or the base for a super sorbet sundae.

3/4 cup graham cracker crumbs
3/4 cup all purpose flour
1 teaspoon baking soda
1/2 teaspoon salt
1/2 cup chopped raisins or dates
3/4 cup soymilk
1 Tablespoon lemon juice
1/4 cup molasses
1/4 cup oil

In a large bowl, combine all ingredients and mix until well blended. Line the bottom of a 8x4-inch or 9x5-inch loaf pan with waxed paper. Pour in the batter. Cover with vented plastic wrap. Microwave on MEDIUM for 5-9 minutes or until bread springs back when touched. Cool at least 5 minutes before slicing.

Total Calories Per Serving: 171   Total Fat as % of Daily Value: 11%
Protein: 2 gm   Fat: 7 gm   Carbohydrates: 26 gm   Calcium: 77 mg
Iron: 2 mg   Sodium: 306 mg   Dietary Fiber: 1 gm

Creamy Ginger
and Date Bread

(Makes 12x8-inch dish or two 8x4-inch loaves (microwave
each loaf separately), approximately 12-14 servings)

This recipe freezes well and can be used as a cake or a
bread.

1 cup all purpose flour
1/4 cup vegan margarine, softened
1/2 cup dry vegan sweetener
4 Tablespoons silken tofu
1/2 cup vegan sour cream or unflavored yogurt
1 teaspoon ground ginger
1/2 teaspoon nutmeg
1/2 teaspoon cinnamon
1/2 teaspoon vanilla extract
1/2 teaspoon baking soda
1/4 teaspoon salt
1/2 cup finely chopped dates
1 Tablespoon molasses

Put all ingredients in a large mixing bowl and blend to
combine. Invert a saucer in the middle of the microwave or
insert a microwave rack. Pour the batter into a 12x8-inch
microwaveable baking dish or shallow casserole or two 8x4-
inch loaves. Microwave on HIGH for 5-8 minutes, or until a
toothpick inserted in the center comes out clean.

Total Calories Per Serving: 139   Total Fat as % of Daily Value: 7%
Protein: 2 gm   Fat: 5 gm   Carbohydrates: 23 gm   Calcium: 41 mg
Iron: 1 mg   Sodium: 151 mg   Dietary Fiber: 1 gm

MUFFINS AND PIES

Muffins "bake" very quickly in the microwave. With a little bit of planning, you can roll out of bed and have hot, steamy blueberry or corn muffins in less than 10 minutes. Prepare the batter ahead of time and store until needed. We've given you a recipe for Make-Ahead Muffins on page 88. Have add-in ingredients, such as chopped nuts, dried fruit, chopped preserved ginger, carob chips, or chopped dried chilies on hand to toss in at will.

To make muffins in a microwave, you'll need muffin papers and small microwave custard cups. I haven't found a plastic or glass microwaveble muffin "tin," but I'm sure they're out there. Custard cups do very well for both microwave muffins and cupcakes. If you don't have custard cups, experiment with small glass coffee cups. If the cups are too large or unevenly shaped, all the batter may not bake evenly.

Guide for Baking Muffins On HIGH Power
> 1 muffin: 30 to 40 seconds
> 2 muffins: 30 seconds to 1-1/2 minutes
> 4 muffins: 1 to 2-1/2 minutes
> 6 muffins 2-1/2 to 4 minutes

Pie fillings can be made in a microwave and some pie-crust can be "baked" in a microwave. Remember, if you want a browned crust, you will not reach your goal with a microwave. Graham cracker and nut crusts work well in a microwave, since the deep color exists in the ingredients. You may want to prepare several piecrusts at a time and refrigerate or freeze them until needed. This makes it easy to prepare a fast dessert, especially during fresh fruit season.

To make a fresh fruit pie, you can peel and slice very ripe fruit, such as peaches or apricots. Prepare a cornstarch slurry (follow the package directions) and mix with a small amount of vegan dry sweetener. Toss the fruit and cornstarch together to coat the fruit, add to a pie shell, and your pie is done. This works well with ripe strawberries, blueberries, a berry and banana combo, raspberries, gooseberries, boysenberries, figs, and plums.

If your microwave is too small to accommodate an entire pie shell, or if you don't need a whole pie, you can cut recipes in half and make individual tarts. If you don't want to bother with piecrust, simply prepare the filling and serve it in individual dishes.

Maple Molasses Bran Muffins

(Makes 5 dozen medium muffins;
each muffin is about 2 ounces)

The batter will keep in the refrigerator for 2-3 weeks. Keep it on hand for last-minute breakfasts or desserts.

2 cups boiling water
2 cups bran flakes cereal (not straight bran)
1 cup molasses
2 cups dry vegan sweetener
1 cup vegan margarine
1 Tablespoon plus 2 teaspoons baking soda
2 teaspoons salt
1/2 cup silken tofu
2 cups all-purpose flour
3 cups soy or rice milk
1 cup maple syrup
3 cups all-purpose flour
4 cups bran flakes cereal

In a large bowl, combine water, 2 cups bran flakes, and molasses. Stir, cover, and set aside.

In a second large bowl, combine sweetener, margarine, baking soda, and salt and mix well. Beat in tofu and mix until well combined. Stir in 2 cups flour. Blend in milk and maple syrup. Add remaining 3 cups flour. Add in the soaked bran flakes and the 4 cups bran flakes. Mix well. Pour muffin batter into plastic or glass containers, cover, date, and refrigerate until ready to use.

To microwave muffins: line a custard cup or small microwave dessert dish with 2 muffin papers. Fill papers half way with muffin batter. Arrange in a circle in the microwave. Microwave according to the chart listed on page 84, allowing approximately 30 seconds for each muffin. Do not microwave more than 6 muffins at a time.

Note: To make oatmeal-bran muffins, replace the 4 cups of bran cereal at the end of the recipe with 4 cups of quick-cooking (not instant) oats.

Total Calories Per Serving: 130 Total Fat as % of Daily Value: 6%
Protein: 2 gm Fat: 4 gm Carbohydrates: 24 gm Calcium: 60 mg
Iron: 1 mg Sodium: 228 mg Dietary Fiber: 1 gm

Make-Ahead Muffins
(Makes 5 dozen muffins)

The mixture for these muffins will last in the refrigerator for 2 weeks. The baked muffins can be frozen and microwaved to reheat when ready to eat.

4 cups whole grain dry cereal
2 cups bran cereal (such as 100% bran flakes)
2 cups hot water
2 cups soy or rice milk
2 cups silken tofu or unflavored soy yogurt
1 Tablespoon lemon juice
3 cups vegan dry sweetener
3/4 cup oil
5 cups all purpose flour
5 teaspoons baking soda
1 teaspoon salt

Place both types of cereal in a large bowl. Pour hot water over cereal. Stir in remaining ingredients. Stir until just blended (you don't want to over stir). Refrigerate until ready to use.

When time to bake, place 6 doubled paper muffin papers on a large plate. Fill each muffin cup half way with batter. Microwave on HIGH for 2-1/2 to 3 minutes or until set. Remove and place on a rack to cool.

Total Calories Per Serving: 120   Total Fat as % of Daily Value: 5%
Protein: 3 gm   Fat: 3 gm   Carbohydrates: 21 gm   Calcium: 13 mg
Iron: 1 mg   Sodium: 155 mg   Dietary Fiber: 1 gm

Corn and Chili Muffins
(Makes 8 muffins)

This moist corn muffin is an excellent accompaniment for bean and chili dishes.

1/2 cup all-purpose flour
1/2 cup cornmeal (yellow gives a better color for microwaving, but white is fine to use)
1/2 cup thawed, frozen cut corn
1/4 cup chopped bell pepper or fresh chilies
1 Tablespoon vegan dry sweetener
2 teaspoons baking powder
1/2 teaspoon salt
1/2 teaspoon chili powder
1/3 cup soymilk
2 Tablespoons silken tofu
1/4 cup oil

Place 2 muffin papers in 8 custard cups or microwave dessert bowls. Fill each paper halfway with the batter. Arrange cups in a ring in the microwave. Refer to the chart on page 84 for microwave cooking time.

Total Calories Per Serving: 139   Total Fat as % of Daily Value: 12%
Protein: 2 gm   Fat: 8 gm   Carbohydrates: 16 gm   Calcium: 73 mg
Iron: 1 mg   Sodium: 274 mg   Dietary Fiber: 1 gm

Peanut Butter Muffins
(Makes 12 muffins)

These muffins could be eaten for breakfast or served for dessert; you decide!

1 cup all-purpose flour
3/4 cup packed brown sugar (you could use any
    other dry vegan sweetener)
1 teaspoon baking powder
1/2 teaspoon salt
1/2 teaspoon vanilla
1/4 cup vegan margarine
3 Tablespoons peanut butter
4 Tablespoons silken tofu
1/2 cup soy or rice milk (you can use vanilla-
    flavored, if desired)

Place all ingredients in a large mixing bowl and blend well, until batter is fluffy. Line custard cups or microwave dessert bowls with 2 muffin papers. Fill each paper 1/3 full. Pull a toothpick or knife through each muffin, to eliminate any air pockets. Arrange in a ring in the microwave. Refer to the chart on page 84 for microwave cooking time. As soon as they are microwaved, remove muffins from custard cups and allow them to cool.

Note: Almond, hazelnut, or other nut butters may be used instead of peanut butter.

Total Calories Per Serving: 148   Total Fat as % of Daily Value: 10%
Protein: 3 gm   Fat: 6 gm   Carbohydrates: 21 gm   Calcium: 40 mg
Iron: 1 mg   Sodium: 189 mg   Dietary Fiber: 1 gm

Ginger Snap Crust

(Makes 9-inch crust; most filled pie shells
can be cut into 6 servings)

Use your extra cookies to make a quick-and-easy pie crust.

1-1/2 cups vegan ginger snap cookies
5 Tablespoons vegan margarine, softened

Smash gingersnaps to form small crumbs. Mix crumbs and margarine well in a 9-inch microwaveble pie pan. Press mixture firmly and evenly into the pan. Microwave on HIGH for 2 minutes. Cool before filling.

Note: Vegan graham crackers can be substituted for the gingersnaps

Total Calories Per Serving: 202   Total Fat as % of Daily Value: 19%
Protein: 2 gm   Fat: 12 gm   Carbohydrates: 22 gm   Calcium: 25 mg
Iron: 2 mg   Sodium: 296 mg   Dietary Fiber: 1 gm

Apple Pie
(Serves 6)

You can use peeled and sliced fresh pears, peaches, or apricots instead of apples. Fresh or frozen berries can be used in place of apples. If berries are extremely juicy, use 3 cups rather than 4 cups.

4 cups peeled and sliced baking apples
2/3 cup vegan dry sweetener
1/2 teaspoon cinnamon
2 Tablespoons flour

Combine all ingredients and mix to combine. Pour into a baked ginger snap or graham cracker crust (see previous page). Set the pie on a piece of waxed paper and microwave on HIGH for 12-14 minutes, or until fruit is tender. Allow pie to cool for 10 minutes before slicing.

Total Calories Per Serving: 133   Total Fat as % of Daily Value: 0%
Protein: <1 gm   Fat: <1 gm   Carbohydrates: 34 gm   Calcium: 23 mg
Iron: 1 mg   Sodium: 8 mg   Dietary Fiber: 2 gm

Raisin Pie
(Serves 6)

Enjoy this unique pie!

2/3 cup vegan dry sweetener
2 Tablespoons cornstarch
1 cup water
2 cups raisins
1/4 cup orange juice
1 Tablespoon orange zest
2 Tablespoons lemon juice
1/2 teaspoon ground ginger

In a 2-quart bowl or casserole, mix sweetener, cornstarch, water, and raisins. Microwave on HIGH for 6 minutes or until thickened, stirring every 2 minutes. Stir in juices, zest, and ginger. Pour into baked shell. Set pie on waxed paper and microwave on MEDIUM for 6 minutes, or until bubbly.

Total Calories Per Serving: 241   Total Fat as % of Daily Value: 0%
Protein: 1 gm   Fat: <1 gm   Carbohydrates: 63 gm   Calcium: 36 mg
Iron: 2 mg   Sodium:24 mg   Dietary Fiber: 3 gm

Many of these recipes can be used for a hot breakfast or for a warm dessert. They taste just as good cold, so prepare some extra servings for the next day.

Scandinavian Dried Fruit Dessert
(Serves 5)

This fruit dessert tastes great on its own or can be served over sorbet, sweetened rice, fresh fruit salad, or cake. It lasts approximately 1 week in the refrigerator.

1-1/2 cups water
1-1/4 cups pitted prunes (about 1/2 pound)
1/4 cup raisins
1/2 cup vegan dry sweetener
1/2 cup chopped walnuts
1 Tablespoon lemon juice
1/4 teaspoon lemon zest
1 teaspoon cinnamon
2 Tablespoons cornstarch

Place water in a 2-quart container and microwave on HIGH for 4 minutes or until boiling. Add prunes and raisins, cover, and let stand for 1 hour.

Drain liquid into a small bowl and leave fruit in the container. Set aside. Stir sweetener, walnuts, juice, zest, cinnamon, and cornstarch into the liquid until well combined. Microwave mixture on HIGH for 2 minutes. Stir well.

Pour mixture over fruit and chill for at least 1 hour before serving.

Note: This dish is traditionally prepared with sweet wine or sherry. If you would like, stir in 1/4 cup sweet dessert wine or sherry before chilling.

Total Calories Per Serving: 291   Total Fat as % of Daily Value: 13%
Protein: 3 gm   Fat: 8 gm   Carbohydrates: 57 gm   Calcium: 60 mg
Iron: 2 mg   Sodium: 14 mg   Dietary Fiber: 5 gm

Quick-Baked Apple
(Serves 1)

Treat yourself to a hot dessert or a hot breakfast item.

1 baking apple (Rome, Cortland, MacIntosh)
3 teaspoons maple syrup
1/2 teaspoon cinnamon
1/2 teaspoon ginger
4 teaspoon cloves
1/2 teaspoon lemon or orange zest
Water to cover

Wash and core apple. Make a 1-inch slice across the top. Place the apple in a 2-cup measure or bowl. Pour the syrup into the cavity left by the core, letting a small amount cover the top of the apple. Sprinkle the spices and zest across the top. Add 1 inch of water to the bottom of the bowl. Microwave on HIGH for 4 minutes or until apple is tender.

Note: Fresh pears can be used as well. Cut off the long slender top of the pear (save it for munching) and proceed as explained above.

Total Calories Per Serving: 168   Total Fat as % of Daily Value: 1%
Protein: 1 gm   Fat: 1 gm   Carbohydrates: 43 gm   Calcium: 53 mg
Iron: 1 mg   Sodium: 8 mg   Dietary Fiber: 6 gm

Mocha Bread Pudding
(Serves 5)

Mmm...mocha!

1/2 cup vegan chocolate or carob chips
1 cup brewed espresso or strong coffee
1 cup soy or rice milk
1 Tablespoon oil or melted vegan margarine
3 Tablespoons silken tofu
1/4 cup vegan dry sweetener
1 teaspoon vanilla extract
1-1/2 cups fresh bread cubes
1/2 teaspoon nutmeg
1/4 teaspoon cinnamon

Place chips in a medium bowl. Cover and microwave on HIGH for 40-60 seconds to soften. Stir in coffee, milk, and oil or margarine. Microwave on HIGH for 3 minutes. Stir in tofu, sweetener, and vanilla.

Put bread cubes in a 1-quart casserole or bowl. Pour mocha mixture over the bread. Sprinkle on nutmeg and cinnamon and toss gently to combine.

To get a steaming effect, place uncooked pudding casserole in a large bowl or casserole. Pour 1 inch of water into the larger bowl or casserole. Microwave on HIGH for 8 minutes or until bubbly. Let stand 5 minutes before serving, or allow pudding to chill completely.

Note: You can use any plain or sweet bread for this recipe, including white, wheat, whole wheat, baguettes, and sweet rolls. Don't use sourdough or breads with caraway seeds, as this is a sweet dessert.

Total Calories Per Serving: 210   Total Fat as % of Daily Value: 15%
Protein: 4 gm   Fat: 10 gm   Carbohydrates: 26 gm   Calcium: 72 mg
Iron: 1 mg   Sodium: 95 mg   Dietary Fiber: 2 gm

Apple Betty
(Serves 6)

This old-fashioned dessert tastes just as good the next day
for breakfast.

5 cups baking apples, peeled, cored, and sliced
   (approximately 2-1/2 pounds)
1/2 cup dry vegan sweetener
1/2 cup raisins, chopped dates, or chopped dried
   figs
1 teaspoon cinnamon
1/4 teaspoon nutmeg
1/4 cup melted vegan margarine
3 cups dried bread cubes, cut into small pieces
1/2 cup water

In a large bowl, combine apples, sweetener, raisins,
cinnamon, and nutmeg. Set aside. In a second bowl, toss
margarine and bread cubes.

   Place half of the apple mixture in the bottom of a 2-quart
bowl or casserole. Top with half of the bread cubes. Repeat
this step. Pour water over mixture. Cover and microwave
on HIGH for 7 minutes. Uncover. Microwave on HIGH for
another 6 minutes or until apples are tender.

Note: You can use fresh pears, peaches, and apricots instead
of the apples in this recipe.

Total Calories Per Serving: 265   Total Fat as % of Daily Value: 13%
Protein: 2 gm   Fat: 9 gm   Carbohydrates: 48 gm   Calcium: 41 mg
Iron: 1 mg   Sodium: 199 mg   Dietary Fiber: 4 gm

Chocolate-Covered Bananas
(Serves 5)

It's fast! It's fun! It's fruit!

5 long wooden skewers or wooden chopsticks
5 peeled bananas
1/2 cup vegan chocolate or carob chips

Skewer each banana down the middle with a wooden skewer. Place on a sheet of waxed paper in the freezer. Place chips in a small bowl and add 2 teaspoons of water.

Microwave on MEDIUM for 2 minutes or until very soft. Remove from microwave and mix to form a smooth sauce. Dip frozen bananas in chocolate to coat. Serve immediately or freeze in waxed paper until ready to use.

Total Calories Per Serving: 202   Total Fat as % of Daily Value: 8%
Protein: 2 gm   Fat: 5 gm   Carbohydrates: 39 gm   Calcium: 52 mg
Iron: 1 mg   Sodium: 18 mg   Dietary Fiber: 5 gm

In the Pantry Biscuits
(Makes about 12 cups of mix; yielding 8 dozen biscuits)

Prepare this refrigerator mix ahead of time and you'll be ready to microwave-bake biscuits just by adding vegan milk.

5 cups all-purpose flour (or half all-purpose and half whole wheat flour)
6 Tablespoons baking powder
1 Tablespoon salt
1-1/2 cups vegan margarine, crumbled into small pieces
5 cups all-purpose flour (or half and half as above)

In a 6-quart bowl, combine 5 cups flour with the baking powder and salt. Mix well. Cut in (mashing with a fork or a pastry cutter) margarine and mix until the dough resembles very fine pebbles. Add in remaining flour and mix until the dough resembles sand. Cover and label and store in the refrigerator or freezer until ready to use.

Notes: This dough should keep in the refrigerator for approximately 3-4 weeks and for several months in the freezer. Each cup of this mix will make approximately 8 biscuits.

Total Calories Per 1-Ounce Serving: 149   Total Fat as % of Daily Value: 18%
Protein: 1 gm   Fat: 11gm   Carbohydrates: 10 gm   Calcium: 57 mg
Iron: <1 mg   Sodium: 297 mg   Dietary Fiber: <1 gm

Ready-to-Bake-Biscuits
(Makes eight 2-inch biscuits)

These biscuits are best eaten hot or warm, since they tend to harden as they cool.

1 cup "In the Pantry" biscuit mix (see previous page)
1/4 to 1/3 cup soy or rice milk (amount will vary)

Place biscuit mix in a large bowl. Add the milk little by little to form a smooth, not sticky, dough. Mix by hand or with a spoon only until combined. If you over-mix, you may not get a high rise from the finished biscuits.

Sprinkle some flour on a cutting board or clean table. Take the dough from the bowl and knead it (work it with your hands) ten times. Roll the dough out to 1/2-inch thickness. Cut out 2-inch diameter biscuits with a round cookie or biscuit cutter or drinking glass. You can also cut the dough into 2-inch squares.

Place the biscuit dough in a circle on a 9-inch plate, a microwave pie plate, or a shallow casserole. You can place dough in the center of the plate, as well. Microwave on HIGH for 2-4 minutes or until puffy and dry. Serve warm.

Total Calories Per Serving: 153   Total Fat as % of Daily Value: 18%
Protein: 2 gm   Fat: 12 gm   Carbohydrates: 11 gm   Calcium: 58 mg
Iron: <1 mg   Sodium: 300 mg   Dietary Fiber: <1 gm

Marmalade Morning Biscuit Cake

(Makes a 9-inch cake or about 9 servings)

Use your favorite flavor of marmalade or jam in this recipe.

Vegetable oil spray
8 Tablespoons graham cracker crumbs
1 cup "In the Pantry" biscuit mix (see page 99)
1/4 cup vegan dry sweetener
2 Tablespoons oil
1/3 cup soy or rice milk (you can use vanilla-
    flavored, if you like)
2 Tablespoons silken tofu
1/2 cup prepared marmalade or jam

To microwave-bake this cake, you'll need to assemble a
baking dish as follows: Spray a 9-inch plate or a microwave
pie pan with oil. Spray a straight glass or plastic microwaveable drinking glass (having about a 3-inch diameter)
with vegetable oil. Place the glass, drinking end up, in the
center of the plate. Sprinkle plate and the base of the glass
with about 3 Tablespoons of graham cracker crumbs.

In a medium-size bowl, combine biscuit mix, sweetener,
oil, milk, and tofu. Mix only until the dry ingredients are
moistened and coated. Drop by spoonfuls around the edge
of the plate. Sprinkle dough with remaining crumbs. Drop 1
teaspoonful of marmalade into the center of each spoonful
of dough. Microwave on HIGH for 3-4 minutes or until the
cake springs back when touched. Remove the glass and
serve warm.

Total Calories Per Serving: 257   Total Fat as % of Daily Value: 22%
Protein: 2 gm   Fat: 14 gm   Carbohydrates: 32 gm   Calcium: 65 mg
Iron: <1 mg   Sodium: 320 mg   Dietary Fiber: <1 gm

Cinnamon Coffee Cake Biscuits

(Makes a high 9-inch cake or about 12 servings)

Preparing a warm, cinnamon coffeecake can be so easy!

2 cups "In the Pantry" mix (see page 99)
2/3 cup soy or rice milk (you can use vanilla-flavored, if you like)
1/2 cup vegan dry sweetener
1/4 cup graham cracker crumbs
1 Tablespoon cinnamon
1/4 cup chopped walnuts or pecans
1/4 cup melted vegan margarine
1/4 cup chopped raisins

In a medium-size mixing bowl, combine the "Pantry" mix and milk only until dough forms. (If the dough is sticky, add another 1-2 Tablespoons of the "Pantry" mix.) In a small bowl, combine sweetener, crumbs, cinnamon, and nuts.

Sprinkle flour on a cutting board or clean table. Knead dough 10 times. Roll out to 1/2-inch thickness. Cut into 2-inch rounds. Lightly brush or roll rounds in margarine and then roll in cinnamon mixture. Arrange rounds on a 9-inch plate or microwave pie plate so they are overlapping approximately 1 inch.

Microwave on HIGH for 4-6 minutes or until cake springs back when touched. Sprinkle with raisins. Allow biscuits to cool for 2 minutes and serve warm.

Total Calories Per Serving: 308   Total Fat as % of Daily Value: 33%
Protein: 3 gm   Fat: 21 gm   Carbohydrates: 27 gm   Calcium: 94 mg
Iron: 1 mg   Sodium: 464 mg   Dietary Fiber: 1 gm

Baking Powder Biscuits

(Makes eight 2-inch biscuits)

This quick, easy recipe almost puts itself together.

1 cup all-purpose flour
1-1/2 teaspoons baking powder
1/4 teaspoon salt
2 Tablespoons vegan margarine
1/3 cup soy or rice milk

Combine flour, baking powder, and salt in a medium-size bowl and mix together. Cut in margarine and combine until dough is crumbly. Add milk slowly, adding only enough to make the dough stick together. Sprinkle a small amount of flour on a cutting board or a clean table. Knead dough ten times. Roll to a 1/2-inch thickness. Cut out in 2-inch rounds or squares. Arrange in a circle on a 9-inch plate or microwave pie pan. Microwave on HIGH for 2-4 minutes or until dry and puffy.

Note: If desired, hot biscuits can be brushed with melted vegan margarine.

Total Calories Per Serving: 86   Total Fat as % of Daily Value: 5%
Protein: 2 gm   Fat: 3 gm   Carbohydrates: 12 gm   Calcium: 55 mg
Iron: <1 mg   Sodium: 199 mg   Dietary Fiber: 1gm

Cripsy Date Bars
(Makes a 9x9-inch pan or approximately 12 bars)

You'll never buy cookies again.

1/2 cup vegan margarine
1 cup vegan dry sweetener
1/3 cup all-purpose flour
1/2 teaspoon salt
4 Tablespoons silken tofu
1 cup whole dates, pitted and cut in half
3 cups crispy rice cereal
1 teaspoon vanilla extract

Place margarine in a 2-quart bowl or casserole and micro-wave on HIGH for 45 seconds, or until melted. Blend in sweetener, flour, salt, and tofu and mix very thoroughly. Stir in dates. Microwave on HIGH for 3-5 minutes or until very thick. Stir every 2 minutes. Allow date mixture to cool for 5 minutes.

Place the cereal and the vanilla extract in a large bowl. Stir in date mixture until all the ingredients are well incorporated. Spread evenly in a 9x9-inch baking pan and allow to chill for at least 1 hour. Cut into small squares (about 1-inch) to serve.

Note: You can use any cold, puffed grain or rice cereal for this recipe.

Total Calories Per Serving: 214   Total Fat as % of Daily Value: 12%
Protein: 1 gm   Fat: 8 gm   Carbohydrates: 36 gm   Calcium: 25 mg
Iron: 1 mg   Sodium: 244 mg   Dietary Fiber: 1 gm

Graham Cracker Toffee Fudge

(Makes a 9x9-inch pan or approximately 12 pieces)

This is a "special treat" recipe that's wonderful to give as a gift.

1 Tablespoon vegan margarine
9 graham cracker squares
1/2 cup vegan margarine
1/2 cup brown sugar or date sugar
1/2 cup sliced almonds
1/2 cup vegan chocolate or carob chips

Place 1 Tablespoon margarine in a 9x9-inch pan and microwave on HIGH for 1 minute. Spread evenly on bottom of pan. Line the pan with the graham crackers so they cover the bottom.

In a 3-cup bowl or casserole, combine 1/2 cup margarine and sugar and microwave on HIGH for 1 minute. Beat with a whisk until smooth. Return to microwave and microwave on HIGH for another 2 minutes. Pour toffee over graham crackers, spreading so it is even. Sprinkle nuts over the toffee. Microwave on high for 1-3 minutes or until toffee boils. Remove from microwave and allow toffee to cool for 3 minutes. Sprinkle chips over nuts. When the chips being to melt, spread them evenly. Store, covered, at room temperature if you want a soft dessert or in the refrigerator for a crisp one.

Total Calories Per Serving: 195   Total Fat as % of Daily Value: 20%
Protein: 2 gm   Fat: 13 gm   Carbohydrates: 18 gm   Calcium: 44 mg
Iron: <1 mg   Sodium: 143 mg   Dietary Fiber: 1 gm

CHAPTER FIVE
Microwave Entrées: Medleys, Curries, and Casseroles

Introduction

Depending on your lifestyle, you may or may not cook a hot entrée for dinner every night. Microwave cooking comes in handy for those times you don't plan to prepare a meal. As long as you have a few ingredients on hand (see Chapter One and Appendix One), you can whip up several entrées in just a few minutes.

You may find that you would like to prepare a dish from the recipes listed on the following pages and freeze half for later use. Or you may cut several recipes in half, and prepare them as a mini-buffet. All the recipes in this chapter will work as hearty appetizers or regular entrées.

How to "Build a Meal" Around an Entrée

If you are planning a meal with appetizers, entrées, and side dishes, you'll want to choose the entrée first. Once you've selected the entrée, it will be easy to coordinate the other dishes you'd like to serve.

When you're planning a meal, consider color, flavor, texture, temperature, and cooking time. For example, creamy mushroom soup, baked tofu tetrazini, mashed potatoes, and cinnamon rice pudding are all good dishes, but they're all the same color and texture. If you'd like to have tofu tetrazini as an entrée, then you might want to have a colorful soup, such as a gazpacho, or a cold, colorful vegetable salad as an appetizer. Side dishes could include sliced orange beets with sweet onions or braised red cabbage. Blueberry pie or pumpkin custard would work well for dessert.

It is feasible to prepare an entire meal in the microwave; it just takes a little choreography and planning. Say you would like to serve curried lentils over couscous as an entrée with a side dish of garlic braised spinach. First, you'd prepare the couscous in the microwave. As the couscous is microwaving, you'll prepare the curried lentils. Remove the couscous from the microwave and keep it covered to hold in warmth. Microwave the lentils. As the lentils are cooking, prepare the spinach, select serving dishes, and set the table. Remove the lentils and stack them on the couscous to keep both containers warm. Microwave the spinach, which will only take 2-3 minutes. Remove the spinach. Immediately place the stacked lentils and couscous in the microwave and heat on HIGH for 2 minutes to perk up the heat. As the lentils and couscous are reheating, stir the spinach and place it in a serving dish or on the table in its microwaved container. When the bell rings, remove the couscous and lentils from the microwave and enjoy a terrific dinner!

Loaves and "Meat" Balls

Many people like to make vegan "meat" balls and "meat" loaf, and both can be made in a microwave. First, review the information in Chapter Three on converting recipes.

Second, find some "meat" ball recipes at the end of this chapter. Finally, unless you have a browning unit, your "meat" balls will taste great but they won't look brown.

Some Microwave Cooking Tips for "Meat" Balls

1. Microwaved "meat" balls freeze well, so plan on doubling or tripling the recipe.

2. For extra flavor, add 1/4 cup sauce or chopped fresh vegetables plus 2 Tablespoons breadcrumbs for every 2 cups of "meat" ball mixture.

3. Be sure to roll the balls uniformly. You can use a measuring spoon or 1/8-1/4 cup measuring cup. Uniform size ensures uniform microwave cooking.

4. Arrange "meat" balls in a single layer in an ungreased shallow casserole. Oil is not necessary, since microwaved "meat" balls will not stick.

5. If you cover the "meat" balls when cooking, use a microwave-safe lid, waxed paper, or plastic wrap. Covering prevents splatters from the sauce.

Basic "Meat" Ball Recipe Variations

Prepare a basic "meat" ball recipe (for example Veggie Balls on page 134), microwave, and drain. You can then choose from the following sauces:

a. Sweet and sour "meat "balls: for a sweet and sour sauce, mix 3/4 cup tomato paste with 2 cups chopped canned tomatoes (not drained), 1/4 cup dry vegan sweetener, 1/4 cup finely chopped green pepper, 1/2 teaspoon ground ginger, 2 Tablespoons vinegar, and 2 teaspoons lemon juice. Mix well. Pour sauce over "meat" balls and microwave.

b. "Secret" ingredient "meat" balls: for a Swedish-influenced "meat" ball sauce, combine 1 cup raspberry or grape preserves with 1 cup ketchup, 1/2 cup tomato paste, 1 Tablespoon grated horseradish, and 2 Tablespoons lemon juice in a medium bowl. Mix well. Microwave on HIGH for 5 minutes or until bubbly. Pour over "meat" ball mixture and microwave.

c. Barbecue "meat" balls: for a fast barbecue sauce, combine 1 cup apple juice, 1/2 cup ketchup or tomato purée, 1/2 cup maple syrup, 4 Tablespoons lemon juice, 1 teaspoon vinegar, 1 teaspoon black pepper, and 1 teaspoon garlic powder in a medium-size bowl. Microwave on HIGH for 5 minutes or until thickened. Pour over "meat" balls and microwave.

d. Teriyaki "meat" balls: for an Asian-influenced dish, combine 1/2 cup prepared teriyaki sauce, 3/4 cup pineapple juice, 1/4 cup maple syrup, 1 Tablespoon orange juice concentrate, 2 minced garlic cloves, 2 teaspoons red pepper flakes, 2 Tablespoons cornstarch, and 1/2 teaspoon ground ginger in a medium-size bowl. Microwave on HIGH for 3 minutes or until thickened. Pour over "meat" balls and microwave.

Cooking Pasta

You can prepare pasta in a microwave. Be very careful — the water and the pasta will get very hot. If possible, use fresh pasta, since it cooks quicker. You cannot save any time by preparing large amounts of pasta in a microwave, so plan on using a microwave to make pasta only when you are preparing a meal that requires 2-3 portions of pasta. Don't try to microwave more than 8 ounces (1 cup) of pasta at a time.

To microwave pasta, put 1 cup pasta in a large glass casserole (at least 7x11-inch) or bowl (3-quart capacity or more). Pour 4 cups boiling water over pasta, so the pasta is covered with water. (You can boil the water in the microwave if you don't have access to a stove.) Cover and microwave on HIGH for 8-10 minutes. Remove from the microwave and let stand, covered, for 3 minutes. Carefully drain the pasta. It's not necessary to rinse the pasta if you are serving it immediately. If you will be serving it later, you'll want to rinse it to prevent sticking. These instructions make 3-4 servings of pasta.

White Cupboard Chili
(Serves 6)

Not your typical "red" chili!

2 cups chopped onion
2 garlic cloves, minced
1 Tablespoon oil
3 cups vegetable broth or stock
1/2 cup white wine (optional)
5 cups canned white beans, drained (try Great
    Northern, Navy, or Cannellini beans)
1/2 cup canned green chilies, drained and chopped
2 Tablespoons fresh chili, deseeded and chopped
2 Tablespoons chopped fresh cilantro
1 teaspoon dried oregano
1 teaspoon dried cumin
1 cup grated vegan cheese or vegan sour cream
    (optional)

In a 3-quart casserole or bowl, combine onions, garlic, and oil. Microwave on HIGH for 3 minutes or until onion is tender. Add remaining ingredients, except cheese or sour cream. Cover with lid or vented plastic and microwave on HIGH for 10 minutes. Stir. Cover and microwave on MEDIUM for 20 minutes or until flavors are combined. If desired, sprinkle on cheese or sour cream before serving.

Total Calories Per Serving Without Cheese or Sour Cream But With Wine: 326
Total Fat as % of Daily Value: 5%
Protein: 17 gm   Fat: 3 gm   Carbohydrates: 55 gm   Calcium: 165 mg
Iron: 4 mg   Sodium: 316 mg   Dietary Fiber: 13 gm

Southwestern-Influenced Rice and Pepper Medley

(Serves 6)

Friends will love this dish.

1 cup chopped onion
1/4 cup chopped green bell pepper
2 Tablespoons fresh chili, deseeded and chopped
1 clove garlic, minced
3 Tablespoons oil
1/2 cup uncooked long grain white rice
2 cups canned stewed tomatoes (with liquid)
1 cup raisins
1/2 cup pine nuts
1 Tablespoon red pepper flakes
1 teaspoon chili powder

In a 2-quart bowl or casserole, combine onions, pepper, chili, garlic, oil, and rice. Microwave on HIGH for 3 minutes. Mix in remaining ingredients. Cover and microwave on HIGH for 8-10 minutes, or until rice is soft and vegetables are tender. Allow dish to stand, covered, for 5 minutes, then fluff with a fork before serving.

Total Calories Per Serving: 297   Total Fat as % of Daily Value: 20%
Protein: 6 gm   Fat: 13 gm   Carbohydrates: 43 gm   Calcium: 52 mg
Iron: 3 mg   Sodium: 201 mg   Dietary Fiber: 5 gm

Taco Salad
(Serves 4)

Combine great textures and flavors for a savory entrée.

1 pound soy crumbles or vegan "ground round"
   (about 2 cups)
1/2 cup chopped onion
16-ounce can kidney beans, drained (or 2 cups
   cooked kidney beans)
1/2 cup water
1 Tablespoon chili powder
1/2 teaspoon cumin
1/2 teaspoon garlic powder
1/2 teaspoon black pepper
1/2 head Romaine lettuce, chopped
1 cup chopped fresh tomatoes
1/2 cup chopped green or red bell pepper
1/2 cup shredded vegan cheese (optional)
1/4 cup sliced black olives
1 cup broken tortilla chips

Combine soy crumbles and onion in a 2-quart bowl or
casserole. Microwave on HIGH for 4 minutes, or until onion
is tender and crumbles are heated through. Add beans,
water, and seasonings. Stir to combine. Cover and microwave on MEDIUM for 10 minutes or until thick and bubbly.
On a serving platter, arrange lettuce, tomatoes, and peppers. Spoon taco mixture over lettuce. Garnish with cheese
(if desired), olives, and chips.

Total Calories Per Serving Without Cheese: 298
Total Fat as % of Daily Value: 6%
Protein: 29 gm   Fat: 4 gm   Carbohydrates: 38 gm   Calcium: 79 mg
Iron: 3 mg   Sodium: 1063 mg   Dietary Fiber: 14 gm

Stuffed Tomatoes Mediterranean

(Serves 4)

This casserole is a traditional Mediterranean dish.

2 large ripe tomatoes
2 slices whole wheat or whole grain bread (remove
   crust)
2 teaspoons nutritional yeast
1 clove garlic, minced
1 teaspoon olive oil
1 teaspoon dried oregano
1 teaspoon dried basil
1/2 teaspoon red pepper flakes
1 teaspoon chopped fresh parsley
2 Tablespoons chopped black olives

Halve tomatoes and gently scoop out pulp, leaving a 2-to 3-inch border. You do not want to take out too much of the tomato pulp, just enough to leave room for some stuffing. Save pulp. Set aside.

In a blender or processor (or by hand) crumble bread, add 1/2 cup tomato pulp, and add remaining ingredients. Process or blend until you have a well-combined, moist mixture.

Place tomato halves in a circle on a 9-inch plate. Fill each tomato half with stuffing. Microwave on HIGH for 10 minutes, or until the stuffing is bubbly and the tomatoes are soft.

Notes: This dish can also be prepared with leftover dinner rolls or corn bread. Sweet onions can be used instead of tomatoes. If you would like a golden-brown finish, preheat oven to 400 degrees and transfer microwaved tomatoes onto a baking sheet. Bake, uncovered for 5 minutes or until golden brown. Extra stuffing can be microwaved, covered, in a small bowl, on HIGH for 8 minutes and served as a side dish.

Total Calories Per Serving: 73   Total Fat as % of Daily Value: 3%
Protein: 3 gm   Fat: 2 gm   Carbohydrates: 13 gm   Calcium: 72 mg
Iron: 1 mg   Sodium: 86 mg   Dietary Fiber: 4 gm

Scrambled Mushrooms with Tofu and Curry
(Serves 3)

This quick dish can be used as a savory breakfast, lunch, or dinner entrée.

1 cup fresh mushrooms, sliced
2 teaspoons curry powder
2 Tablespoons oil
1 cup firm tofu, crumbled

In a 1-quart casserole or bowl, combine mushrooms, curry, and oil. Cover and microwave on HIGH for 4-6 minutes, or until mushrooms are very tender. Carefully mix in tofu. Microwave, uncovered, for 2 minutes or until heated through.

Total Calories Per Serving: 157   Total Fat as % of Daily Value: 20%
Protein: 8 gm   Fat: 13 gm   Carbohydrates: 5 gm   Calcium: 144 mg
Iron: 2 mg   Sodium: 9 mg   Dietary Fiber: 1 gm

Microwave Lasagna

(Serves 6)

Lasagna made simple!

1 pound firm tofu, crumbled (about 2 cups)
1/2 cup chopped onion
1 clove garlic, minced
2 cups canned tomatoes, chopped, drained (saving
    1/2 cup juice)
1/4 cup chopped fresh parsley
2 teaspoons dried oregano
2 teaspoons dried basil
1-3/4 cups soft tofu
1/2 cup grated vegan soy cheese
1 teaspoon black pepper
10 no-cook lasagna noodles (see note)
1-3/4 cups tomato sauce
2 cups grated vegan soy cheese

Combine firm tofu, onion, and garlic in a 2-quart casserole and microwave on HIGH for 2 minutes or until the onion is just tender. Add tomatoes, parsley, oregano, and basil. Microwave on HIGH for 3 minutes. Stir.

In a medium bowl, combine soft tofu, 1/2 cup soy cheese, reserved tomato juice, and black pepper, and mix until combined.

In a microwave casserole, layer 1/3 of the noodles, 1/3 of the sauce, and 1/3 of the tofu mixture. Repeat two more times. Top with 2 cups grated soy cheese.

Microwave on MEDIUM (50%) for 20-30 minutes or until bubbly. Let stand for 10 minutes before cutting.

Note: If no-cook lasagna noodles are not available, micro-wave regular lasagna noodles before beginning to prepare lasagna. Place 2 teaspoons oil and 5 cups hot tap water into a 12x8-inch or 9x9-inch microwave casserole. Cover tightly with plastic wrap and microwave on HIGH for 5 minutes or until water boils. Uncover and add noodles. Cover tightly and microwave on HIGH for 5 minutes or until noodles are *al dente* (tender, but firm). Rinse well under cold water and allow noodles to drain on paper towels.

Total Calories Per Serving: 257   Total Fat as % of Daily Value: 7%
Protein: 12 gm   Fat: 5 gm   Carbohydrates: 43 gm   Calcium: 134 mg
Iron: 4 mg   Sodium: 452 mg   Dietary Fiber: 4 gm

Spinach Lasagna

(Serves 5)

It's easy being green with this pasta recipe.

10-ounce package frozen chopped spinach (about
   1-1/2 cups)
1 pound extra firm tofu, crumbled (about 2 cups)
1/4 cup chopped onion
1 teaspoon garlic powder
15 ounces prepared spaghetti sauce
1/4 cup breadcrumbs
1/2 cup silken tofu
1 teaspoon black pepper
1 cup shredded vegan cheese

Place spinach package on a paper towel in the microwave
and microwave on HIGH for 3 minutes or until defrosted.
Drain in a colander and set aside. In a 2-quart bowl or
casserole, combine extra firm tofu, onion, and garlic powder. Microwave on HIGH for 2 minutes. Stir in sauce. Cover
and microwave on HIGH for 2 more minutes or until bubbly. Mix in breadcrumbs.

In a small bowl, combine spinach, silken tofu, and black
pepper. In a 9x9-inch casserole or square baking pan,
spread half the tomato sauce mixture. Cover with all the
spinach mixture. Sprinkle with cheese. Top with remaining
tomato sauce mixture. Microwave on HIGH for 5 minutes
or until heated through.

Total Calories Per Serving: 248   Total Fat as % of Daily Value: 17%
Protein: 15 gm   Fat: 11 gm   Carbohydrates: 25 gm   Calcium: 193 mg
Iron: 4 mg   Sodium: 741 mg   Dietary Fiber: 4 gm

Summer Squash and Eggplant Stew (Ratatouille)

(Serves 6)

This is a traditional vegetable stew from Southern France.

3 cups fresh zucchini, sliced thin (about 2 medium zucchini)
1-1/2 cups sliced onion, separated into rings (about 1 large onion)
3 cups peeled eggplant, cut into small cubes
2 Tablespoons olive oil
2 teaspoons chopped fresh basil
1 teaspoon dried oregano
2 teaspoons chopped fresh parsley
1 garlic clove, minced
2 cups chopped, canned tomatoes, drained

In a 3-quart casserole, combine all ingredients, except tomatoes. Cover and microwave on HIGH for 8 minutes. Stir in tomatoes, re-cover casserole, and microwave for 10 minutes, or until vegetables are tender.

Total Calories Per Serving: 99   Total Fat as % of Daily Value: 7%
Protein: 3 gm   Fat: 5 gm   Carbohydrates: 13 gm   Calcium: 51 mg
Iron: 2 mg   Sodium: 131 mg   Dietary Fiber: 4 gm

Baked Eggplant

(Serves 4)

Better make a double batch of this dish!

3/4 cup chopped onion
1 teaspoon garlic powder
1/2 cup chopped green bell pepper
2 teaspoons olive oil
3/4 cup tomato paste (6-ounce can)
1/2 cup tomato juice
1 teaspoon vegan dry sweetener
1/2 teaspoon dried oregano
1/2 teaspoon dried basil
2-1/2 cups eggplant (about 1 medium eggplant)
1 cup shredded vegan cheese

In a 2-quart casserole or bowl, combine onion, garlic, pepper, and olive oil. Microwave on HIGH for 2-3 minutes or until vegetables are tender. Stir in tomato paste, juice, sweetener, oregano, and basil. Microwave on HIGH for 3 minutes or until bubbly. Stir and set aside.

Wash unpeeled eggplant and cut into small cubes. Place the eggplant cubes in the bottom of an 8x8-inch baking dish or flat casserole. Cover with wax paper or a lid. Microwave on HIGH for 6 minutes or until eggplant is tender. Sprinkle half the cheese over the eggplant. Spoon the tomato sauce over the cheese. Finish by sprinkling the remaining cheese on top of the tomato sauce. Microwave on HIGH for 4 minutes or until cheese melts and the casserole is heated thoroughly.

Total Calories Per Serving: 179   Total Fat as % of Daily Value: 9%
Protein: 4 gm   Fat: 6 gm   Carbohydrates: 29 gm   Calcium: 21 mg
Iron: 2 mg   Sodium: 707 mg   Dietary Fiber: 4 gm

Vegan Kishka

(Makes about 14 slices, or 7 servings)

A traditional recipe for a vegetable sausage, updated for the microwave; serve over broad noodles or with mashed potatoes and mushroom gravy. This dish freezes well.

2 cups large diced onion
1 cup large diced carrot
1/4 cup chopped celery
1/4 cup chopped green pepper
1/4 cup silken tofu
1/4 cup oil
2 cups matzo meal or finely crumbled matzo
1/4 cup vegetable stock or water
1 teaspoon garlic powder
1 teaspoon black pepper
2 teaspoons paprika

Place onion, carrots, celery, and green pepper into the canister of a food processor or a blender. Process until you have a fine mixture—i.e., cannot distinguish individual pieces of vegetable. Add remaining ingredients and process until well combined.

Place mixture into a shallow round casserole or glass pie plate (9-inch diameter). Shape mixture into a round. Cover with waxed paper. Microwave on HIGH for 3 minutes, or until firm. Allow kishka to stand for 3 minutes before slicing.

Total Calories Per Serving: 191   Total Fat as % of Daily Value: 13%
Protein: 4 gm   Fat: 8 gm   Carbohydrates: 27 gm   Calcium: 24 mg
Iron: 2 mg   Sodium: 29 mg   Dietary Fiber: 3 gm

Mushroom Pasta
(Serves 5)

Take advantage of all the different types of fresh mushrooms available for this iron-rich dish.

4 cups pre-cooked pasta, your choice (or conventionally cook 1-1/2 cups raw pasta)
1-1/4 pounds fresh mushrooms, sliced (approximately 2-1/2 cups)
1/4 cup chopped celery
1/4 cup chopped onion
1 clove garlic, minced
1 Tablespoon olive oil
2 cups canned chopped tomatoes, drained (saving 1/2 cup liquid)
1 Tablespoon chopped fresh parsley (or 2 teaspoons dried parsley)
1 Tablespoon chopped fresh basil (or 2 teaspoons dried basil)
1 teaspoon dried oregano
3/4 cup tomato paste

If cooking pasta, drain and allow pasta to cool.

Combine mushrooms, celery, onion, and garlic with oil in a 2-quart bowl or casserole. Cover and microwave on HIGH for 4 minutes or until vegetables are tender.

Add remaining ingredients and stir to combine. Cover. Microwave on MEDIUM for 15 minutes or until sauce is thickened. Stir in pasta and serve immediately.

Total Calories Per Serving: 262   Total Fat as % of Daily Value: 7%
Protein: 10 gm   Fat: 4 gm   Carbohydrates: 48 gm   Calcium: 56 mg
Iron: 5 mg   Sodium: 512 mg   Dietary Fiber: 5 gm

Vegan Sausage and Creamy Potatoes

(Serves 4)

This is a hearty dish with lots of texture and taste.

4 medium boiling potatoes, peeled and sliced
   (about 1-1/2 pounds)
1/4 cup water
1/3 cup vegan cream cheese
1/2 cup soymilk
1 Tablespoon flour
2 Tablespoons chopped green onions
1/2 teaspoon dry mustard
1/2 teaspoon white pepper
1 teaspoon caraway seeds
1 cup sliced vegan sausage or vegan hot dog

Combine potatoes and water in a 2-quart casserole or bowl. Cover and microwave on HIGH for 6 minutes or until potatoes are tender (flake with a fork). Drain, return to bowl, and set aside.

Place cream cheese in a 2-cup bowl or measure and microwave on HIGH for 20 seconds or until softened. Stir in soymilk, flour, mustard, pepper, and caraway seeds. Pour sauce over potatoes and gently mix to combine. Arrange sliced sausage on top of potatoes. Cover and microwave on HIGH for 4 minutes or until heated through.

Total Calories Per Serving: 176   Total Fat as % of Daily Value: 2%
Protein: 14 gm   Fat: 1 gm   Carbohydrates: 28 gm   Calcium: 23 mg
Iron: 2 mg   Sodium: 374 mg   Dietary Fiber: 4 gm

Teenie Beenie Weenies, Updated
(Serves 5)

I can remember eating this dish as a child.

1/2 cup chopped red apple (not peeled)
1/2 cup chopped onion
1 Tablespoon vegan margarine
1 Tablespoon cornstarch
Two 16-ounce cans kidney beans, drained (or 4
    cups cooked kidney beans)
16-ounce can vegetarian baked beans
1/2 pound vegan hot dogs, sliced (about 1-1/4
    cups)
2 Tablespoons molasses
2 Tablespoons vinegar
1 Tablespoon apple juice concentrate
1/2 teaspoon prepared mustard
8-ounce can pineapple chunks, drained

Combine apple, onion, margarine, and cornstarch in a 2-quart bowl or casserole. Microwave on HIGH for 2 minutes or until onion is tender. Add remaining ingredients. Microwave on HIGH for 8 minutes or until sauce is thickened and ingredients are heated through. Serve warm.

Total Calories Per Serving: 462   Total Fat as % of Daily Value: 6%
Protein: 30 gm   Fat: 4 gm   Carbohydrates: 82 gm   Calcium: 129 mg
Iron: 2 mg   Sodium: 746 mg   Dietary Fiber: 25 gm

Fast "Fried" Rice
(Serves 4)

This rice is much lower in fat than the type made in restaurants.

1/2 cup chopped green onions
1/4 cup chopped celery
1/4 cup chopped green pepper
1 teaspoon oil
1 cup long-grain rice
1-3/4 cups vegetable broth
1 teaspoon soy sauce

Put onions, celery, and pepper in a 2 quart bowl or casserole and toss with oil. Microwave on HIGH for 3 minutes or until vegetables are still crisp. Add remaining ingredients. Cover and microwave on HIGH for 5 minutes or until boiling. Reduce to MEDIUM and microwave for 10 minutes or until all the liquid is absorbed and rice is cooked.

Total Calories Per Serving: 201   Total Fat as % of Daily Value: 2%
Protein: 4 gm   Fat: 1 gm   Carbohydrates: 41 gm   Calcium: 26 mg
Iron: 2 mg   Sodium: 296 mg   Dietary Fiber: 2 gm

Spanish-Style Rice
(Serves 4)

This dish is colorful and flavorful; pair with a fresh salad and a toasty baguette.

1 clove garlic, minced
3/4 cup chopped onion
1/4 cup chopped green pepper
1 Tablespoon oil
1 cup long-grain rice
1 cup vegetable broth
1 cup prepared tomato sauce
1 teaspoon black pepper
1/2 teaspoon dried oregano

Place garlic, onion, green pepper, and oil in a 2-quart bowl or casserole. Microwave on HIGH for 4 minutes. Add remaining ingredients and cover. Microwave on HIGH for 5 minutes. Stir and reduce heat to MEDIUM. Microwave for 10 minutes or until all liquid is absorbed and rice is cooked.

Total Calories Per Serving: 242   Total Fat as % of Daily Value: 6%
Protein: 5 gm   Fat: 4 gm   Carbohydrates: 46 gm   Calcium: 34 mg
Iron: 3 mg   Sodium: 490 mg   Dietary Fiber: 3 gm

Rice Casserole
(Serves 6)

Enjoy this iron-rich hearty casserole! If you are on a lowfat diet, note that this recipe is high in fat.

1/4 cup oil
1 cup chopped onion
2 cups long-grain rice
1/2 cup pine nuts
3-3/4 cups boiling vegetable stock (you'll need to do this on the stove)
1/2 cup raisins
1/2 cup canned chopped tomatoes, drained
1/4 cup chopped fresh parsley
1/2 cup chopped pistachio nuts

Place oil in a 3-quart bowl or casserole. Add onions and microwave on HIGH for 6 minutes or until tender. Stir in rice and pine nuts. Microwave on HIGH for 4 minutes. Add boiling stock and raisins. Cover and microwave on HIGH for 6 minutes or until boiling. Reduce to MEDIUM as soon as the mixture comes to a boil and microwave for 10 more minutes or until all the liquid is absorbed. Stir in tomatoes, parsley, and pistachios, cover, and let stand for 10 minutes before serving.

Total Calories Per Serving: 500   Total Fat as % of Daily Value: 31%
Protein: 11 gm   Fat: 20 gm   Carbohydrates: 71 gm   Calcium: 50 mg
Iron: 5 mg   Sodium: 328 mg   Dietary Fiber: 4 gm

Barley and Mushroom Casserole

(Serves 4)

You'll find all the comforts of home in one dish.

1/2 cup chopped onion
1 cup sliced fresh mushrooms
1 Tablespoon oil
1/4 cup grated carrot
1 cup pearled barley
2 cups hot vegetable stock
1 Tablespoon fresh parsley
1 teaspoon garlic powder

Combine onions and mushrooms with oil in a 2-quart bowl or casserole. Microwave on HIGH for 3 minutes or until vegetables are tender. Add remaining ingredients and cover. Microwave on HIGH for 4 minutes or until boiling. As soon as the mixture is boiling, reduce to MEDIUM and microwave for 30 minutes or until tender. Let stand covered for 10 minutes before serving.

Total Calories Per Serving: 238   Total Fat as % of Daily Value: 6%
Protein: 6 gm   Fat: 4 gm   Carbohydrates: 46 gm   Calcium: 23 mg
Iron: 2 mg   Sodium: 239 mg   Dietary Fiber: 9 gm

Bulgur Pilaf
(Serves 4)

Enjoy a hint of Morocco in this dish.

1/2 cup chopped dried apricots
1/2 cup raisins
1/2 cup vegetable stock
1/2 cup chopped onion
1/4 cup chopped celery
2 teaspoons oil
1 cup bulgur (cracked wheat)
1-1/4 cups vegetable stock
1 Tablespoon chopped fresh parsley
1/2 cup chopped pine nuts or walnuts

Combine apricots and raisins in a 2-cup bowl or measure. Add 1/2 cup stock and microwave on HIGH for 1-2 minutes or until very hot. Set aside.

In a 2-quart casserole or bowl, combine onion, celery, and oil and microwave on HIGH for 2 minutes or until vegetables are tender. Stir in bulgur, 1-1/4 cups vegetable stock, and parsley. Cover and microwave on HIGH for 12 minutes or until liquid is absorbed. Let stand for 5 minutes. Stir in apricots and raisins. Garnish with chopped pine nuts.

Total Calories Per Serving Using Pine Nuts: 347
Total Fat as % of Daily Value: 18%
Protein: 10 gm   Fat: 12 gm   Carbohydrates: 56 gm   Calcium: 38 mg
Iron: 4 mg   Sodium: 217 mg   Dietary Fiber: 7 gm

Reuben-Style Sandwich
(Makes 1 sandwich)

See how fast you can assemble this sandwich!

3 vegan deli slices
2 slices rye bread
2 Tablespoons sauerkraut, drained
1 slice vegan cheese
2 teaspoons Thousand Island dressing (see notes)

Assemble sandwich by placing deli slices on one slice of bread, followed by sauerkraut and cheese. Spread dressing on second slice of bread and cover sandwich. Place sandwich on a plate and microwave for 40 seconds or until sandwich is hot.

Notes: You can purchase a vegan brand of Thousand Island dressing or prepare your own Thousand Island dressing by mixing 1 teaspoon of vegan mayonnaise with 1 teaspoon of ketchup. Also, you may want to skewer the sandwich with toothpicks or wrap it in a paper towel to keep it together while heating.

Total Calories Per Serving: 318   Total Fat as % of Daily Value: 11%
Protein: 18 gm   Fat: 7 gm   Carbohydrates: 45 gm   Calcium: 53 mg
Iron: 2 mg   Sodium: 1221 mg   Dietary Fiber: 4 gm

Toasted Peanut and Apple Sandwich

(Makes 1 sandwich)

This is Elvis' second favorite sandwich.

2 Tablespoons creamy peanut butter
1 Tablespoon applesauce
2 slices white or wheat bread

Assemble sandwich by spreading one slice of bread with peanut butter and topping with applesauce. Cover with second slice of bread. Wrap in a paper towel. Microwave on HIGH for 2 minutes or until heated through.

Total Calories Per Serving: 326
Protein: 13 gm   Fat: 18 gm
Iron: 2 mg   Sodium: 414 mg

Total Fat as % of Daily Value: 28%
Carbohydrates: 31 gm   Calcium: 65 mg
Dietary Fiber: 4 gm

Tofu Balls with Sauerkraut and Mustard
(Makes about 20 tofu balls)

Enjoy a little taste of Oktoberfest in a tofu ball.

Vegetable oil spray
1-1/2 pounds firm tofu, crumbled into tiny pieces
1 cup diced onion
1-1/3 cups canned or fresh sauerkraut, well drained
1 teaspoon dried mustard
1/4 cup soymilk
1/4 cup tomato paste
1 cup breadcrumbs
1 Tablespoon paprika

Spray a shallow pan with vegetable oil spray. Add tofu, onions, sauerkraut, and mustard and microwave on HIGH for 2 minutes or until onions are soft.

Place mixture in a blender canister and add soymilk and tomato paste. Blend for 1 minute or until just combined. Add breadcrumbs and paprika and blend for 30 seconds or until just combined (if overblended, mixture will not hold shape).

Roll mixture into about 20 balls. Spray a plate or baking pan with oil; place balls in single layer on the plate and microwave on HIGH for 5-6 minutes or until firm. Repeat until all tofu balls are cooked.

Serve warm, with a mustard or mushroom sauce.

Total Calories Per Serving: 58   Total Fat as % of Daily Value: 3%
Protein: 4 gm   Fat: 2 gm   Carbohydrates: 7 gm   Calcium: 68 mg
Iron: 1 mg   Sodium: 221 mg   Dietary Fiber: 1 gm

Mushroom and Hazelnut Snacking Balls

(Serves 6)

Serve these as an appetizer or pair with broad noodles or angel hair pasta as an entrée.

Vegetable oil spray
1/2 medium onion, chopped
1 cup chopped fresh button mushrooms
2 cloves garlic, minced
1 cup hazelnuts (also called filberts)
1/4 cup chopped fresh parsley
1 teaspoon soy sauce
1/2 teaspoon onion powder
2 teaspoons nutritional yeast
1 teaspoon cracked black pepper

In a shallow pan or plate, spray vegetable oil. Add onion, mushrooms, and garlic and microwave for 3 minutes on HIGH or until mushrooms and onion are soft. Place vegetables and all remaining ingredients into a blender or food processor and blend until smooth. Mixture will be very thick. Form into small balls or patties and refrigerate for at least 30 minutes before serving. Can be served cold or heated briefly (about 30 seconds on HIGH) in the microwave.

Total Calories Per Serving: 134   Total Fat as % of Daily Value: 18%
Protein: 4 gm   Fat: 12 gm   Carbohydrates: 6 gm   Calcium: 32 mg
Iron: 1 mg   Sodium: 59 mg   Dietary Fiber: 2 gm

Veggie Balls
(Serves 6)

This one is a great "pantry" recipe because many of the ingredients should already be on your shelf. It's also a terrific way to use leftover veggies and is high in iron. Serve with mashed potatoes and corn on the cob for a hearty meal.

16-ounce can (or 1-1/2 cups) sliced carrots, drained (saving liquid)
16-ounce can (or 1-1/2 cups) cut green beans, drained
1-1/2 cups cooked pinto or red beans
2-1/2 cups dry breadcrumbs
2 Tablespoons vegetable oil or melted vegan margarine
1 Tablespoon dried parsley
1/2 cup ketchup or chili sauce
2 Tablespoons silken tofu
1/2 teaspoon white pepper
1/2 teaspoon celery salt
1 teaspoon onion powder
Vegetable oil spray

Place carrots, green beans, and pinto beans in a blender or food processor and purée until almost smooth. Place mixture in a large bowl. Stir in remaining ingredients until well combined. If mixture is too thick, add some of the reserved carrot liquid; if it is too thin, add additional breadcrumbs.

Roll mixture into small balls. Spray a plate or shallow pan with oil. Place balls on the plate and microwave on HIGH for 4 minutes or until firm. Repeat until all the balls are cooked.

Note: This mixture can be pressed into a loaf pan and microwaved on HIGH for 5 minutes as a loaf or pressed into patties and fried or baked as burgers.

Total Calories Per Serving Using Oil: 321   Total Fat as % of Daily Value: 10%
Protein: 11 gm   Fat: 7 gm   Carbohydrates: 55 gm   Calcium: 106 mg
Iron: 4 mg   Sodium: 2152 mg   Dietary Fiber: 7 gm

CHAPTER SIX
Microwave Appetizers and Side Dishes

It seems as if most people these days don't find time to sit down and have a "constructed" meal. You know, soup, followed by salad, then an entrée accompanied by a starch and a veggie, ending with dessert. "Leave it to Beaver" mealtimes are far and few between so far in the twenty-first century.

In this chapter you will find appetizers and side dishes that can be mixed and matched to create whole meals. In fact, "grazing," or ordering multiple appetizers or side dishes instead of entrées, is a popular restaurant trend. Now you can be fashionable in your own kitchen using your own microwave.

When it comes to vegetables and fruit, take advantage of the seasons. In the summer, bring home soft-shelled squash, like zucchini and yellow squash, tomatoes, fresh green and wax beans, corn, snow peas, peaches, apricots, and berries for your microwave. In the autumn, you'll find seasonal fresh greens, fresh beans, apples, pears, carrots, beets, cabbage, potatoes, and onions to work with. In the winter, you'll probably find a lot of root vegetables, such as turnips, rutabagas, and parsnips and hard squash in the fresh produce section. You may want to supplement your fresh winter produce with frozen and dried varieties. They all have a place in the microwave.

Pointers to Make Your Life Easier

1. Quick frozen veggies: Place 1/2 cup frozen vegetables in a plastic or glass dish or bowl. Cover with vented plastic or lid and microwave on HIGH for 2 minutes. Most vegetables will create their own broth, so there's no need to add water. You may have to drain some excess water from high-liquid containing veggies, such as spinach and Brussels sprouts.

2. Fresh carrots for one or two: Fresh vegetables take very little time in the microwave. You only need to wash, peel, and slice them. If you're really pressed for time, you can purchase precut fresh vegetables. When ready to go, slice 1 cup of fresh carrots. Place them in a plastic or glass dish or bowl. Add 1 Tablespoon of water. Cover and cook on MEDIUM for 5-6 minutes, or until tender. That's it! Toss with some fresh or dried herbs or some vegan margarine and you have terrific fresh veggies.

Appetizers can be assembled in a hurry when you're using a microwave. Treat yourself to a dinner "buffet" of several appetizers rather than one entrée. For example, if you would like to make fast and furious nachos, we recommend the *open-and-pile* method: open a bag of baked tortilla chips and pile on a microwaveable dinner plate. Open a can of vegetarian refried beans and pile the beans on top of the chips. If you've got some olives, open them, slice, and pile them on top of the beans. To continue, open a bag of veggie sliced cheese, crumble, and pile on top of the olives. Place your masterpiece in the microwave and cook on HIGH for 2 minutes or until the cheese is melted and the beans are hot. Open the microwave and, voila! You'll have fast and slightly nutritious nachos. This method works with any kind of chip, such as pita chips or veggie chips. If you have a little more time and some leftover beans, you can mash them instead of using the canned beans. You can add your own accents, such as chopped onions, salsa, chopped tomatoes, sliced fresh or pickled chilies, fresh parsley or cilantro, or chopped bell peppers.

Another variation on this theme would be using canned, drained artichokes (packed in brine or water, NOT marinated), hearts of palm, canned baby corn or canned asparagus, and croutons instead of chips for the base. Top the artichokes or other vegetables with a small amount of vegan mayonnaise, then shredded vegan cheese, then olives...you get the idea.

Quick-cooking rice obviously cooks the fastest in a microwave, but may lack flavor or texture. See Chapter Eight for microwave rice cooking techniques. It's always a good idea to cook more rice than you need, as it is very versatile. Cooked rice can be combined with nuts, spices, herbs, and chopped vegetables or dried fruit and quickly microwaved to create wonderful, hot side dishes or entrées.

For example, we like to combine cooked long-grain rice with chopped cashews, chopped green onions, a shake of garlic powder, and a splash of soy sauce, then cover and microwave for fast "fried" rice. Cooked rice can be moistened with canned tomato or mushroom soup and chopped bell peppers and microwaved. Wash and chop the amount of greens that will fit in a large microwave bowl. Fill bowl with about one inch of water. Cover and microwave until greens are wilted. Drain, toss with a little garlic or onion powder, and you've got fast microwave greens.

Spicy Toasted Nachos

(Makes 8 large servings)

This dish can be a fast lunch or dinner, or the beginning of a great meal.

3 cups baked tortilla chips (7-ounce bag)
1 cup grated vegan cheese
1/2 cup vegan sour cream
1/2 cup prepared salsa
1/2 cup chopped fresh tomatoes, or canned, drained tomatoes
1/4 cup frozen, thawed cut corn or canned, drained cut corn
2 teaspoons hot sauce or Tabasco

Place chips on a microwave-safe platter in a single layer. Sprinkle grated cheese evenly over chips. Drop sour cream by Tablespoons over cheese. In a cup, combine salsa, tomatoes, corn, and hot sauce. Pour evenly over sour cream. Microwave on HIGH for 2 minutes or until cheese melts. Serve hot.

Total Calories Per Serving: 144   Total Fat as % of Daily Value: 4%
Protein: 4 gm   Fat: 3 gm   Carbohydrates: 29 gm   Calcium: 6 mg
Iron: <1mg   Sodium: 190 mg   Dietary Fiber: 2 gm

Stuffed Mushrooms or Cherry Tomatoes

(Makes about 24 pieces)

This dish can be served as an appetizer, as a side dish, or as a garnish for an entrée. These can be eaten hot or cold.

24 large, fresh button mushrooms or cherry
    tomatoes
1-1/4 cups frozen chopped spinach, thawed
1/4 cup chopped green onions
1 Tablespoon minced fresh basil (or 2 teaspoons
    dried basil)
1/2 cup firm tofu, drained and crumbled
1 Tablespoon silken tofu
2 teaspoons black pepper

Clean mushrooms or tomatoes. If using mushrooms, twist off stems to create a mushroom cap. For tomatoes, thinly slice off top of tomatoes and scoop out the pulp. You can reserve the mushroom stems or the tomato pulp for another use, such as in a salad or soup.

Squeeze spinach so as much excess liquid is removed as possible. Discard liquid. In a blender or food processor canister, place spinach, onions, basil, firm tofu, silken tofu, and pepper and process until just mixed. This mixing can also be done by hand.

Place a paper towel on a 9-inch plate or platter. Fill mushrooms or tomatoes so they are slightly mounded. Place on plate, arranging them in a circle. Cover very loosely with a paper towel. Microwave on HIGH for 2 minutes or until filling is steaming.

Note: It may take more than one plate to prepare this dish, depending on the size of the mushrooms or tomatoes.

Total Calories Per Serving Using Mushrooms: 10
Total Fat as % of Daily Value: 0%
Protein: 1 gm   Fat: <1 gm   Carbohydrates: 1 gm   Calcium: 20 mg
Iron: <1mg   Sodium: 8 mg   Dietary Fiber: <1 gm

Individual Microwave Pizzas

(Makes 4 individual pizzas)

Make extra of this quick and easy dish and enjoy the next day for breakfast or lunch.

2 English muffins, split in half
3/4 cup prepared tomato or pizza sauce
1/2 cup chopped green pepper
1/4 cup chopped green onions
1/4 cup sliced fresh mushrooms
1/2 cup chopped fresh tomatoes
1/4 cup black olives, drained and sliced
3/4 cup shredded vegan soy cheese

Toast muffins in a regular toaster. Allow muffins to cool. Assemble pizzas by placing a Tablespoon of sauce on each half, followed by an assortment of vegetables and topping each half with 2 Tablespoons of cheese. Place on a dinner plate (9-inch diameter), about one inch apart. Microwave on HIGH for 3 minutes or until cheese has melted.

Notes: If you would like to make a different number of pizzas, allow about 30 seconds per pizza. Other ingredients you might consider to top your pizza with are canned, drained black or red beans, fresh or frozen (thawed) chopped spinach, canned, chopped artichoke hearts, drained capers, chopped red or sweet onion, minced fresh garlic, canned, drained chopped pineapple, or chopped, cooked veggie sausages or burgers.

Total Calories Per Serving: 172   Total Fat as % of Daily Value: 7%
Protein: 4 gm   Fat: 5 gm   Carbohydrates: 29 gm   Calcium: 71 mg
Iron: 2 mg   Sodium: 550 mg   Dietary Fiber: 3 gm

Vegan Chopped Liver
(Makes 6 small appetizer portions)

Make enough of this recipe to go around and around again. People can't seem to stop eating it.

2 cups frozen thawed green beans (or canned, drained green beans)
1/4 cup extra firm tofu, drained
1-1/2 cups minced onion
3 Tablespoons oil
1/3 cup walnuts, finely chopped
2 teaspoons black pepper
2 Tablespoons vegan mayonnaise

Place green beans in a small bowl and set aside. Cut tofu into small cubes and mix with beans. In a small bowl, combine onion and oil, and microwave on HIGH for 5 minutes or until tender. Place all ingredients in the canister of a blender or processor and chop until you have a fine paste. Place on a plate or platter and shape into a log or a round. Refrigerate at least 2 hours before serving.

Total Calories Per Serving: 162   Total Fat as % of Daily Value: 21%
Protein: 3 gm   Fat: 14 gm   Carbohydrates: 9 gm   Calcium: 39 mg
Iron: 1 mg   Sodium: 26 mg   Dietary Fiber: 3 gm

Baked Potatoes

(Serves 4)

If you have a microwave and a potato, a hot meal is never far away.

4 medium baking potatoes (about 2 pounds)

Scrub potatoes well and allow them to dry. Pierce potatoes in 4-5 places with a fork. On your turntable or on a round plate, arrange potatoes in a circle, about one inch apart, with the narrow ends facing inward. Microwave on HIGH, uncovered, for 5 minutes. Stop microwave and turn potatoes over. Microwave for 4 more minutes or until tender. Remove from the microwave and let stand for 3 minutes, so the steam will escape. The potatoes will remain hot for a while, so use care when cutting into them.

Notes: If cooking only one potato, reduce cooking time to 3 minutes at first and then 4 minutes. If potatoes are large, they may take up to 15 minutes to bake in the microwave. Leftover baked or "boiled" potatoes may be cut into large chunks, sprinkled with your favorite herb mixture, and brushed with olive oil then microwaved until hot for a fast appetizer or side dish.

Total Calories Per Serving: 133   Total Fat as % of Daily Value: 0%
Protein: 3 gm   Fat: <1 gm   Carbohydrates: 31 gm   Calcium: 12 mg
Iron: 2 mg   Sodium: 10 mg   Dietary Fiber: 3 gm

"Boiled" Potatoes

(Serves 4)

Hardly any water is needed for this quick and easy dish!

6 red rose or white rose boiling potatoes (about
    1-1/2 pounds or 3 cups)
2 Tablespoons cold water

Wash potatoes, peel, and cut into large chunks. Place potatoes in a 2-quart microwave bowl or casserole and sprinkle with water. Cover with a microwave-safe lid or plastic wrap with holes poked in it. Microwave on HIGH for 5 minutes. Remove potatoes, shake to rotate and mix potatoes. Microwave on HIGH for 4 minutes longer or until tender.

Let potatoes stand for 3 minutes before serving.

Notes: A good rule of thumb is to allow about 5 minutes for each pound of potatoes. Be sure to cook some extra potatoes and store them in the refrigerator to use in other recipes.

Total Calories Per Serving: 120   Total Fat as % of Daily Value: 0%
Protein: 2 gm   Fat: 0 gm   Carbohydrates: 30 gm   Calcium: 0 mg
Iron: 0 mg   Sodium: 60 mg   Dietary Fiber: 2 gm

Mashed Potatoes

(Serves 4)

This is a quick comfort food that's good for breakfast, lunch, dinner, or a snack.

3 cups "boiled" potatoes (see previous recipe)
1/2 cup soymilk or vegan soy sour cream
2 teaspoons vegan margarine
1 teaspoon white pepper

In a microwave-safe bowl or casserole, mash hot "boiled" potatoes with a fork or potato masher until completely mashed. Add milk, margarine, and pepper, and mix well. Cover and microwave on HIGH for 1 minute to warm potatoes.

Note: For a very lowfat version, use 1/2 cup lowfat vegetable broth and eliminate the soymilk and margarine. Allow dish to microwave for 30 additional seconds.

Total Calories Per Serving Using Soymilk: 150
Total Fat as % of Daily Value: 3%
Protein: 4 gm   Fat: 2 gm   Carbohydrates: 32 gm   Calcium: 4 mg
Iron: <1 mg   Sodium: 90 mg   Dietary Fiber: 3 gm

Mashed Potatoes with Rutabagas
(Serves 4)

Maximize the sweetness of the potatoes with the sharpness of the rutabaga in this recipe.

1/2 pound fresh rutabaga, peeled and cut into small cubes (about 1 cup)
1 baking potato, peeled and cut into small cubes (about 3/4 cup)
1 teaspoon oil
1 teaspoon white pepper
1/4 teaspoon ground nutmeg

Place rutabagas in a 2-quart casserole or bowl. Add 1/2 cup water, cover, and microwave on HIGH for 10-12 minutes or until rutabagas are fork-tender—i.e., fall apart easily with a fork. Add potatoes, cover, and microwave for 5 minutes on HIGH until potatoes are fork tender.

Drain rutabagas and potatoes, and save liquid. Add oil, pepper, and nutmeg and mash with a potato masher or fork. Add reserved liquid, as needed, to make a moist product. When mashed and well combined, cover and return to microwave. Microwave on HIGH for 3 minutes or until steamy.

Total Calories Per Serving: 47   Total Fat as % of Daily Value: 2%
Protein: 1 gm   Fat: 1 gm   Carbohydrates: 8 gm   Calcium: 20 mg
Iron: <1 mg   Sodium: 9 mg   Dietary Fiber: 2 gm

Stuffed Baked Potatoes
(Serves 4)

This dish works as an entrée, side dish, or appetizer.

4 baked potatoes (see recipe on page 144)
2 Tablespoons vegan margarine
1/3 cup vegan soy sour cream or unflavored soy
   yogurt
1 teaspoon white pepper
1/4 cup grated vegan soy cheese
1/4 cup chopped green onions
1/4 cup sliced black olives (optional garnish)

When baked potatoes are cool enough to handle, cut them in half lengthwise. Scoop out the centers, saving potato pulp and leaving a half-inch border of potato around the skins.

In a small bowl, combine potato pulp with margarine, sour cream or yogurt, pepper, cheese, and green onions, and mix well.

Place potato skins on a microwave platter. Stuff each skin with the potato mixture. Microwave on HIGH for 3 minutes or until very hot.

Notes: Stuffed potatoes freeze well, so make some extra. Do not thaw when ready to reheat. Just take them from the freezer, place in microwave, and cover with plastic wrap with several holes in it (or waxed paper) then microwave on HIGH for 3 minutes. Reposition potatoes (move them around) and microwave for 3 more minutes. When micro-waving stuffed potatoes, allow about 45 seconds per potato half.

Total Calories Per Serving Without Olives: 193
Total Fat as % of Daily Value: 7%
Protein: 4 gm   Fat: 5 gm   Carbohydrates: 36 gm   Calcium: 40 mg
Iron: 3 mg   Sodium: 137 mg   Dietary Fiber: 3 gm

Pizza Potatoes
(Serves 6)

A twist on two favorites!

4 baked potatoes (see recipe on page 144)
1 cup prepared pizza sauce or tomato sauce
1/4 cup chopped onion
1/4 cup chopped green bell pepper
1/4 cup sliced fresh or canned mushrooms
1/4 cup chopped fresh or canned (drained)
    tomatoes
1/4 cup grated vegan soy cheese (optional)

Cut baked potatoes in half, lengthwise, and scoop out slightly (just enough room to add veggies). You can eat the potato pulp or save it for later use.

Arrange potato halves on a microwave-safe round plate. Spoon about 2 Tablespoons of sauce into each half. Top each half equally with remaining ingredients. Spoon 1 Tablespoon of sauce on top of each potato.

Microwave on HIGH for 2-1/2 minutes. Rotate potatoes and microwave for 30 more seconds.

Total Calories Per Serving Without Cheese: 123
Total Fat as % of Daily Value: 1%
Protein: 3 gm   Fat: 1 gm   Carbohydrates: 26 gm   Calcium: 20 mg
Iron: 2 mg   Sodium: 198 mg   Dietary Fiber: 3 gm

Hot Potato and Caraway Salad (Vegan German Potato Salad)

(Serves 4)

This version is tangy and hot, with no mayonnaise needed.

1/4 cup water
4 medium boiling potatoes, peeled and quartered
  (about 1 pound or 2-1/2 cups)
2 teaspoons oil
1/2 cup chopped onion
1 Tablespoon dry vegan sweetener
1 Tablespoon flour
2 teaspoons caraway seeds
1/2 teaspoon black pepper
2 Tablespoons crumbled vegan bacon strips
  (optional)
1/2 cup water
1/4 cup vinegar

Place potatoes in a 2-quart container. Add water, cover, and microwave on HIGH for 10 minutes or until tender. Set aside.

In a small bowl, combine oil and onion, and mix. Microwave for 1 minute or until tender. Stir in sweetener, flour, caraway, pepper, and vegan bacon strips (if desired). Microwave for 30 seconds. Stir in water and vinegar and microwave for 3 minutes or until mixture is thickened.

Slice potatoes without removing them from the bowl. Pour sauce over and gently combine. Microwave for 1-2 minutes or until hot.

Note: Traditional German potato salad is served hot, flavored with bacon. We have used vegan bacon strips to add a smoky flavor.

Total Calories Per Serving Without "Bacon": 128
Total Fat as % of Daily Value: 4%
Protein: 3 gm   Fat: 3 gm   Carbohydrates: 25 gm   Calcium: 23 mg
Iron: 1 mg   Sodium: 89 mg   Dietary Fiber: 2 gm

Orange Rice with Celery
(Serves 5)

Pair this rice with teriyaki-infused grilled broccoli or steamed tofu.

1 cup chopped celery
1/4 cup chopped onion
2 Tablespoons oil
2 Tablespoons orange juice concentrate
2 cups cooked rice

In a 1-quart bowl, mix together celery, onion, and oil. Microwave on HIGH for 2 minutes or until vegetables are tender. Stir in orange juice concentrate. Mix in rice. Cover and microwave on HIGH for 6-8 minutes or until heated through.

Total Calories Per Serving: 163   Total Fat as % of Daily Value: 9%
Protein: 2 gm   Fat: 6 gm   Carbohydrates: 26 gm   Calcium: 16 mg
Iron: 1 mg   Sodium: 21 mg   Dietary Fiber: <1 gm

Sweet Potatoes in Orange Shells

(Serves 6)

This recipe looks beautiful on the table.

3 large oranges (to be juiced)
6 orange shells (halves from orange juice)
4 medium sweet potatoes (about 1-1/2 pounds)
2 teaspoons vegan margarine
3/4 cup fresh orange juice (from oranges above)
2 Tablespoons cinnamon
1/2 teaspoon powdered ginger
1/4 teaspoon ground cloves
1/4 teaspoon fresh orange zest

Cut oranges in half and juice them. You should measure 3/4 cup orange juice. If you don't have enough, supplement with packaged orange juice. Scoop out orange halves and save the shells.

Wash sweet potatoes and prick in several spots. Place potatoes on a paper towel and microwave on HIGH for 12-15 minutes or until very soft.

Peel potatoes. (Be careful!) Scoop potato pulp into a large bowl. Mash with margarine, orange juice, orange juice concentrate, cinnamon, ginger, cloves, and zest. Mash and mix until smooth.

Set orange shells into a casserole or microwaveable serving platter with high sides (to hold the oranges upright). Fill shells with potato mixture. Microwave on HIGH for 5 minutes or until warm.

Total Calories Per Serving: 180   Total Fat as % of Daily Value: 3%
Protein: 3 gm   Fat: 2 gm   Carbohydrates: 40 gm   Calcium: 91 mg
Iron: 2 mg   Sodium: 16 mg   Dietary Fiber: 7 gm

Creamy Garlic Rice with Parsley and Onions
(Serves 4)

If not used as a side dish this rice can be paired with baked tofu, grilled vegetables, or barbecued seitan.

2 cups cooked rice (See Chapter Eight on how to
   prepare rice in a microwave)
1 Tablespoon chopped green onions
3 Tablespoons olive oil
1 clove garlic, chopped
1/2 teaspoon black pepper
3 Tablespoons silken tofu
1 cup soymilk
2 Tablespoons chopped fresh parsley or
   1 Tablespoon dried parsley flakes

Combine rice, onions, oil, garlic, and pepper in a 1-quart casserole or bowl. In a small bowl, mix together tofu and milk. Stir into rice. Microwave on HIGH for 10 minutes or until heated through. Mix in parsley right before serving.

Total Calories Per Serving: 240   Total Fat as % of Daily Value: 18%
Protein: 5 gm   Fat: 12 gm   Carbohydrates: 29 gm   Calcium: 14 mg
Iron: 2 mg   Sodium: 10 mg   Dietary Fiber: 1 gm

Spinach Rice with Almonds
(Serves 6)

A complement to seasoned black beans or to braised greens.

3 cups cooked rice
2 cups fresh spinach, firmly packed, shredded (or
  thawed, drained frozen chopped spinach)
1/2 cup chopped green onions
1/4 cup chopped fresh parsley
1/2 cup sliced or slivered almonds
2 Tablespoons oil
2 teaspoons lemon juice
2 Tablespoons silken tofu
1 cup soymilk
2 teaspoons white pepper

In a 2-quart bowl or casserole, combine rice, spinach, onion, parsley, almonds, oil, and lemon juice. In a small bowl, whisk together tofu, milk, and pepper. Stir into rice. Cover and chill for 30 minutes to allow mixture to absorb moisture. With the cover still on, microwave dish on HIGH for 12-15 minutes or until heated through.

Total Calories Per Serving: 253
Protein: 7 gm   Fat: 11 gm
Iron: 3 mg   Sodium: 24 mg

Total Fat as % of Daily Value: 18%
Carbohydrates: 32 gm   Calcium: 65 mg
Dietary Fiber: 3 gm

Creamy Spinach
(Serves 3)

Better make a double batch of this recipe; everybody will want seconds.

10-ounce package frozen spinach
2 teaspoons oil
1 Tablespoon all purpose or unbleached white flour
1/8 teaspoon nutmeg
1/8 teaspoon white pepper
1/2 cup silken tofu

Place frozen spinach in a 1-quart bowl or measure. Cover and microwave on HIGH for 5-6 minutes or until thawed. Set aside.

Place oil in a small cup or bowl. Stir in flour, nutmeg, and pepper. Blend in tofu. Microwave on HIGH for 1-2 minutes or until thickened.

Drain spinach in a colander or strainer. Return to bowl. Mix in sauce and microwave on HIGH for 1 minute to heat.

Total Calories Per Serving: 82   Total Fat as % of Daily Value: 7%
Protein: 5 gm   Fat: 4 gm   Carbohydrates: 7 gm   Calcium: 119 mg
Iron: 2 mg   Sodium: 72 mg   Dietary Fiber: 3 gm

Double Orange Carrots

(Serves 5)

This dish is both colorful and flavorful.

4 cups fresh carrots, cut lengthwise into thin 3-inch
   strips
1 Tablespoon oil
1-1/4 cups canned Mandarin orange sections,
   drained
2 teaspoons orange juice concentrate
1 teaspoon powdered ginger

Place carrots and oil in a 1-quart bowl or casserole and stir
to combine. Microwave on HIGH for 8 minutes or until
carrots are tender. In a small bowl, combine Mandarin
oranges, concentrate, and ginger. Add to carrots and stir to
combine. Microwave on HIGH for 2 minutes.

Total Calories Per Serving: 98   Total Fat as % of Daily Value: 4%
Protein: 1 gm   Fat: 3 gm   Carbohydrates: 17 gm   Calcium: 35 mg
Iron: 1 mg   Sodium: 34 mg   Dietary Fiber: 3 gm

Baked Corn, Baked Bean Style
(Serves 5)

Who says only beans can benefit from maple syrup and mustard?

3/4 cup tomato purée
2 Tablespoons maple syrup
1 teaspoon dry mustard
1/4 cup chopped onion
3 cups canned corn, drained (or fresh corn, cut
    from the cob)

In a 2-quart casserole or bowl, combine purée, syrup, dry mustard, and onion. Stir to combine. Add corn and mix to combine. Microwave on HIGH for 5 minutes or until mixture is bubbly.

Note: Canned or fresh corn work best with this recipe. (Frozen corn toughens up and does not absorb the sauce well.)

Total Calories Per Serving: 122
Protein: 3 gm   Fat: 1 gm
Iron: 1 mg   Sodium: 361 mg

Total Fat as % of Daily Value: 2%
Carbohydrates: 28 gm   Calcium: 20 mg
Dietary Fiber: 3 gm

Parsley and Soy Cauliflower
(Serves 5)

This dish will impress the guests! The whole head of cauli-flower is cooked in one piece, making an edible centerpiece.

1 medium head cauliflower, trimmed of outer leaves
   (about 2 pounds)
1/2 cup chopped green onion
2 Tablespoons chopped fresh parsley or cilantro
1 Tablespoon oil
1 cup vegetable broth or stock
1 Tablespoon cornstarch
1 Tablespoon soy sauce

Wash cauliflower and place in 2-quart casserole or bowl. Cover with a lid or vented plastic and microwave on HIGH for 8 minutes or until tender. Remove from microwave and drain, if necessary. Return to casserole and set aside.

In a small cup or bowl combine onion, parsley, and oil. Cover and microwave on HIGH for 2 minutes or until onions are tender. Set aside.

Place broth in small cup or bowl and microwave on HIGH for 1 minute to heat. Remove from the microwave and stir in cornstarch and soy sauce, mixing until smooth. Combine onion and broth.

Pour sauce over cauliflower and microwave on HIGH for 2 minutes, to heat. Remove, place on a serving platter, and serve hot.

Total Calories Per Serving: 72   Total Fat as % of Daily Value: 4%
Protein: 3 gm   Fat: 3 gm   Carbohydrates: 10 gm   Calcium: 26 mg
Iron: 1 mg   Sodium: 331 mg   Dietary Fiber: 3 gm

Cranberry Winter Squash
(Serves 2)

This dish can be enjoyed as a side dish or a dessert!

1 large acorn squash
1/4 cup fresh cranberries
3 Tablespoons maple syrup
1/2 teaspoon ground cinnamon
1/2 teaspoon ground ginger
1 teaspoon lemon zest

Wash squash and cut in half. Scoop out seeds and discard.

In a small bowl, combine cranberries, syrup, cinnamon, ginger, and zest, and mix. Place squash on a microwaveable dish and fill with the cranberry mixture. Microwave on HIGH for 8-10 minutes or until squash is soft and cranberries are tender.

Total Calories Per Serving: 175   Total Fat as % of Daily Value: 0%
Protein: 2 gm   Fat: <1 gm   Carbohydrates: 45 gm   Calcium: 99 mg
Iron: 2 mg   Sodium: 10 mg   Dietary Fiber: 4 gm

Golden Carrots

(Serves 4)

This dish brings exotic flavors to good ol' carrots.

3/4 cup golden raisins
1 cup hot water (from the tap)
2 cups thinly sliced, peeled carrots
1 cup vegetable stock or broth
3 teaspoons fresh ginger, minced
1 teaspoon lemon juice
1 teaspoon orange juice concentrate
2 teaspoons cornstarch
1 teaspoon lemon zest

In a 2-cup bowl, combine raisins and hot water. Microwave on HIGH for 2 minutes. Set aside.

In a 2-quart bowl or casserole, combine carrots, stock, ginger, and lemon juice. Cover and microwave on HIGH for 8-10 minutes or until carrots are tender.

Drain raisins and reserve liquid. In a small bowl, combine orange juice concentrate, cornstarch, lemon zest, and 1/4 cup raisin liquid. Stir until smooth. Add raisins to carrots. Pour sauce over carrots and stir. Cover and microwave on HIGH for 2 minutes or until sauce is warm.

Total Calories Per Serving: 136   Total Fat as % of Daily Value: 0%
Protein: 2 gm   Fat: <1 gm   Carbohydrates: 34 gm   Calcium: 34 mg
Iron: 1 mg   Sodium: 140 mg   Dietary Fiber: 3 gm

Garlic Spinach with Sesame
(Serves 5)

This flavorful and colorful dish goes well with "fried" rice.

2 pounds frozen chopped spinach, thawed and
  squeezed of excess liquid (discard liquid)
2 Tablespoons sesame seeds
1 clove garlic, minced
1 Tablespoon oil

Place spinach in a 3-quart casserole or bowl. Microwave, uncovered, for 1 minute on HIGH. Remove from microwave and squeeze to remove more liquid. Place back in the cooking container and toss with sesame seeds, garlic, and oil. Microwave, uncovered, on HIGH for 5 minutes or until spinach is hot.

Note: For toasted sesame seeds, spray a small frying pan with vegetable oil and allow to heat. Place sesame seeds in pan and allow dish to toast over high heat, stirring to avoid sticking, for about 2 minutes.

Total Calories Per Serving: 89   Total Fat as % of Daily Value: 8%
Protein: 6 gm   Fat: 5 gm   Carbohydrates: 8 gm   Calcium: 238 mg
Iron: 4 mg   Sodium: 135 mg   Dietary Fiber: 6 gm

Soy Sauce Broccoli with Garlic and Hazelnuts
(Serves 4-6)

Enjoy this broccoli as a side dish or an entrée, paired with steamed udon noodles or whole wheat pasta.

1 pound chopped fresh broccoli or frozen, thawed
  chopped broccoli (about 2-1/2 cups)
2 teaspoons sesame or peanut oil
1/4 cup green onions, chopped
2 cloves garlic, minced
2 teaspoons low sodium soy sauce
2 Tablespoons hazelnuts, coarsely chopped

In a 2-quart bowl or casserole, place broccoli and 1/4 cup cold water. Cover and microwave on HIGH for 3 minutes or until broccoli is just tender. Drain, put back in bowl, and set aside.

In a small bowl, combine oil, onions, garlic, soy sauce, and hazelnuts. Toss to combine. Add sauce to broccoli and toss. Microwave on HIGH for 1 minute, to warm just slightly.

Total Calories Per Serving: 80   Total Fat as % of Daily Value: 7%
Protein: 4 gm   Fat: 5 gm   Carbohydrates: 8 gm   Calcium: 66 mg
Iron: 1 mg   Sodium: 121 mg   Dietary Fiber: 4 gm

Green Steamed Kohlrabi
(Serves 4)

Use the bulbs of green, purple, or white kohlrabi. If you have kohlrabi leaves left, save them to use as cooked greens.

2 pounds fresh kohlrabi, peeled, leaves removed, and cut matchstick-style
1 cup vegetable stock or broth
1 teaspoon dried dill
1 teaspoon black pepper

Place kohlrabi in a 2-quart bowl or casserole. Add stock. Cover and microwave on HIGH for 10-12 minutes or until the kohlrabi is tender. Add dill and pepper, then stir and serve.

Total Calories Per Serving: 71   Total Fat as % of Daily Value: 0%
Protein: 4 gm   Fat: <1 gm   Carbohydrates: 16 gm   Calcium: 61 mg
Iron: 1 mg   Sodium: 161 mg   Dietary Fiber: 8 gm

Coriander Kale with Slivered Carrots

(Serves 4)

Kale cooks very quickly in the microwave.

1 pound fresh kale (about 4 cups)
1/2 cup hot water (from tap)
1/2 cup peeled carrots cut matchstick-style
1 clove garlic, minced
2 teaspoons dried coriander
1 Tablespoon oil

Rinse and drain kale. Remove stems from each leaf. Stack several leaves on top of each other and cut into thin strips, as if to make confetti. Place in 3-quart bowl or casserole, add water, and microwave uncovered on HIGH for 4 minutes or until kale is tender. Drain and place back into bowl. Add carrots, garlic, coriander, and oil. Toss well to combine. Microwave uncovered on HIGH for 1 minute, only to warm. Carrots will be crunchy when served.

Total Calories Per Serving: 75   Total Fat as % of Daily Value: 6%
Protein: 3 gm   Fat: 4 gm   Carbohydrates: 9 gm   Calcium: 103 mg
Iron: 1 mg   Sodium: 34 mg   Dietary Fiber: 2 gm

Beet Greens and Green Onions
(Serves 5)

Beet greens are "spicier" than their milder cousins, collard and kale. You may want to mix several greens together in this recipe for a milder taste.

3 cups fresh beet greens
1/2 cup sliced green onions
1 teaspoon black pepper

Wash and drain beet greens. Chop into small pieces, resembling chopped spinach. Place in a 3-quart bowl or casserole and add water so it is 1 inch up on the side of the cooking container. Microwave, uncovered, on HIGH for 3 minutes or until greens are tender. Drain and return to cooking container. Add onions and pepper and toss to combine. Microwave, uncovered, on HIGH for 1 minute, only to warm.

Total Calories Per Serving: 8   Total Fat as % of Daily Value: 0%
Protein: 1 gm   Fat: <1 gm   Carbohydrates: 2 gm   Calcium: 35 mg
Iron: 1 mg   Sodium: 48 mg   Dietary Fiber: 1 gm

Okra Bayou
(Serves 4)

Vegan flavor hits the Big Easy in this dish.

1 teaspoon olive oil
1/4 cup chopped onion
1 clove garlic, minced
1/4 cup chopped green bell pepper
1/2 cup chopped fresh tomato
1/2 pound fresh okra or frozen okra, thawed, sliced
1 teaspoon dried oregano
1/2 teaspoon dried thyme
1/2 teaspoon black pepper
1/2 teaspoon red pepper flakes
1 dash hot sauce or Tabasco

In a 2-quart casserole or bowl, combine olive oil, onion, and garlic. Microwave on HIGH for 2 minutes or until onion is tender. Add green pepper and microwave on HIGH for 30 seconds. Add tomato and okra, cover, and microwave on HIGH for 7-9 minutes or until tomatoes and okra are tender. Add spices and microwave uncovered on HIGH for 1 minute.

Total Calories Per Serving: 44   Total Fat as % of Daily Value: 2%
Protein: 2 gm   Fat: 1 gm   Carbohydrates: 8 gm   Calcium: 61 mg
Iron: 1 mg   Sodium: 9 mg   Dietary Fiber: 3 gm

Orange Snow Peas with Cashews

(Serves 5)

Enjoy this dish as an appetizer, side dish, or as an entrée paired with stir-fried seitan or steamed brown rice.

3 cups fresh snow peas (edible pea pods) or sugar
   snaps, washed
2 teaspoons fresh orange zest
1 teaspoon oil
1 teaspoon white pepper
2 Tablespoons chopped cashews

In a 1-quart bowl or casserole, combine snow peas, zest, and oil. Microwave for 2 minutes on HIGH or until the snow peas are crunchy, yet tender. Stir in pepper and cashews, microwave on HIGH for 30 seconds, then serve.

Note: If fresh snow peas are not available, frozen, thawed snow peas may be used. Reduce initial cooking time to 1 minute.

Total Calories Per Serving: 46   Total Fat as % of Daily Value: 4%
Protein: 2 gm   Fat: 3 gm   Carbohydrates: 5 gm   Calcium: 20 mg
Iron: 1 mg   Sodium: 2 mg   Dietary Fiber: 1 gm

Snow Peas with Pine Nuts
(Serves 2)

This dish is fast to make and a good source of iron!

1/2 pound fresh or frozen, thawed snow peas
1/2 cup pine nuts
1 teaspoon lemon juice

If using fresh snow peas, string and remove caps, if desired. Place in a 1-quart bowl. Cover and microwave on HIGH for 2 minutes. Drain. Return to bowl and stir in remaining ingredients.

Total Calories Per Serving: 241 | Total Fat as % of Daily Value: 27%
Protein: 11 gm Fat: 17 gm | Carbohydrates: 14 gm Calcium: 58 mg
Iron: 5 mg Sodium: 6 mg | Dietary Fiber: 4 gm

Oktoberfest Sweet and Sour Red Cabbage with Green Apples
(Serves 5)

Combine this hearty side dish with grilled vegan sausage or vegan hot dogs on crusty rolls for an Autumn flavorfest.

1 cup apple cider or juice
3 Tablespoons apple cider vinegar or white vinegar
1/2 teaspoon allspice
1/4 teaspoon cloves
1/4 teaspoon onion powder
3 cups shredded fresh red cabbage
1 cup grated green apple (leave peel on)

In a 3-quart casserole or bowl, combine cider, vinegar, all-spice, cloves, and onion powder. Cover and microwave on HIGH for 3 minutes or until mixture comes to a boil. Stir in cabbage and apples. Microwave on HIGH, uncovered, for 10-15 minutes or until cabbage is tender and flavors are combined.

Total Calories Per Serving: 51   Total Fat as % of Daily Value: 0%
Protein: 1gm   Fat: <1 gm   Carbohydrates: 13 gm   Calcium: 24 mg
Iron: <1 mg   Sodium: 9 mg   Dietary Fiber: 2 gm

Cabbage and Caraway
(Serves 4)

This dish is similar to traditional fresh sauerkraut.

4 cups shredded green cabbage
2 Tablespoons water or vegetable broth
2 teaspoons vegan margarine
2 Tablespoons silken tofu
1 teaspoon caraway seeds

Place cabbage in a 2-quart casserole or bowl. Add water and margarine. Cover and microwave on HIGH for 6 minutes or until cabbage is tender. Drain and return to bowl. Stir in tofu and seeds. Microwave on HIGH for 30 seconds to 1 minute until heated through.

Total Calories Per Serving: 41   Total Fat as % of Daily Value: 4%
Protein: 2 gm   Fat: 2 gm   Carbohydrates: 4 gm   Calcium: 40 mg
Iron: 1 mg   Sodium: 35 mg   Dietary Fiber: 2 gm

Brussels Sprouts Mediterranean

(Serves 4)

If Brussels sprouts are not available, you can use quartered fresh kohlrabi bulbs. The cooking time will be the same.

1-1/2 cups frozen Brussels sprouts
2 Tablespoons water
1/4 cup chopped green onions
1 Tablespoon olive oil
3 teaspoons lemon juice
1 teaspoon dried basil
1/2 teaspoon dried oregano
1/2 teaspoon fennel seeds

Combine Brussels sprouts and water in a 2-quart bowl or casserole. Cover and microwave on HIGH for 7 minutes or until thoroughly defrosted. Set aside.

In a small bowl, combine onion and oil. Microwave on HIGH for 1 minute or until onions are tender. Stir in juice and spices.

Drain Brussels sprouts and return to the bowl. Pour onion mixture over sprouts and mix to combine. Microwave on HIGH for 30 seconds to 1 minute or until heated thoroughly.

Total Calories Per Serving: 49
Protein: 1 gm   Fat: 4 gm
Iron: 1 mg   Sodium: 5 mg
Total Fat as % of Daily Value: 5%
Carbohydrates: 4 gm   Calcium: 20 mg
Dietary Fiber: 2 gm

Peas with Mushrooms and Onions

(Serves 4)

This dish is very retro, very 50's, very fun.

1/4 cup chopped onion
2 teaspoons oil
10-ounce package frozen peas (or 1-1/2 cups)
1/2 cup canned mushrooms, pieces and stems,
    drained (4-ounce can)
1/4 teaspoon sage

Toss onion and oil together in a 1-quart casserole or bowl. Cover and microwave on HIGH for 1-2 minutes or until onions are tender. Stir in remaining ingredients. Cover and microwave on HIGH for 5 minutes or until peas are heated thoroughly.

Note: Peas are used in their frozen form in this recipe to provide extra liquid.

Total Calories Per Serving: 86   Total Fat as % of Daily Value: 4%
Protein: 5 gm   Fat: 3 gm   Carbohydrates: 12 gm   Calcium: 18 mg
Iron: 1 mg   Sodium: 184 mg   Dietary Fiber: 4 gm

Easy Zucchini
(Serves 3)

We like to make this recipe with different types of summer squash. It's easy and it's very flavorful.

1 pound sliced fresh zucchini (about 3 medium zucchini)
2 Tablespoons vegan Italian or vinaigrette salad dressing

Put zucchini in a 2-quart casserole or bowl. Toss zucchini with salad dressing. Cover and microwave on HIGH for 5 minutes or until tender.

Note: This recipe works with summer squash, sweet onions, tomatoes, and mushrooms. For extra flavor, toss the vegetables with the salad dressing and allow to stand in a refrigerator for 1-8 hours before microwaving.

Total Calories Per Serving: 73   Total Fat as % of Daily Value: 8%
Protein: 2 gm   Fat: 5 gm   Carbohydrates: 7 gm   Calcium: 30 mg
Iron: 1 mg   Sodium: 83 mg   Dietary Fiber: 2 gm

Whole Spaghetti Squash
(Serves 5)

Gather your guests around when you start to get the "pasta" from the squash.

1 whole spaghetti squash, 2-3 pounds

When purchasing your squash, be sure it will fit in your microwave and rotate. Also make sure you know the weight of your squash. (Most produce sections have scales available.) Wash and dry it well. Pierce in many places, all over the squash, with a fork or knife.

Place the squash on a microwave-safe rack. Microwave on HIGH for 5 minutes per pound. The average spaghetti squash takes about 15 minutes to cook. To ensure even cooking, turn the squash over halfway through cooking. When the squash is done, it will still be firm, but give slightly to the touch. Remove from the microwave and wrap in a clean kitchen towel. Let it stand for 5 minutes so the internal steam can dissipate.

Once the squash has cooled, you can check for doneness with a knife. The knife should cut easily through. If this is not the case, return the squash to the microwave for additional cooking.

Cut the squash in half, lengthwise. Remove seeds and discard. Pull a fork gently through the squash to separate the "spaghetti" strands.

Season your squash "pasta" with pepper and vegan margarine or toss with tomato sauce.

Total Calories Per Serving: 56   Total Fat as % of Daily Value: 2%
Protein: 1 gm   Fat: 1 gm   Carbohydrates: 13 gm   Calcium: 42 mg
Iron: 1 mg   Sodium: 31 mg   Dietary Fiber: 3 gm

CHAPTER SEVEN
Microwave Soups, Dips, and Dressings

Introduction

Microwaves are great for making soups from scratch and for reheating prepared soups. Frozen soups reheat in a matter of minutes and retain their texture and flavor. You can also prepare cooked ingredients in the microwave to be added to soup simmering on the stove.

Soups and sauces especially concentrate heat, so always use a potholder. Don't let a little time lapse fool you. When covered, microwaved soups stay hot after cooking for at least 15 minutes. Use caution when opening lids and moving containers of hot microwave soups and sauces. You can get just as much of a steam burn from microwaved foods as from conventionally cooked foods.

One serving (about 1 cup) of refrigerated soup takes about 2-3 minutes to reheat on HIGH. Be sure to stir at least once for even heating. Soups freeze well. To make life easy, freeze soups in microwaveable containers in the size you usually serve, so you can take the soup directly from the freezer and put it right in the microwave. Defrost soup on HIGH until partially thawed, stirring several times. If you have frozen soup in a non-microwave-safe container, first place the container in hot water to loosen the contents and then transfer it into a microwave safe container for defrosting and reheating.

Making canned or ready-to-use soups in the microwave is a snap. There's no need for having cold meals anymore. Just combine a can of condensed soup (usually 10 ounces) in a large bowl or cup. Mix with one can of water, soymilk, or rice milk and stir. Microwave on HIGH for 5 minutes or until bubbly. You'll end up with approximately 2 servings.

If you have a dry soup mix, use a large bowl. Mix one packet (or 4 servings of dry soup mix) with the amount of hot water called for on the packet. Cover with a lid or vented plastic wrap and microwave on HIGH for 5 minutes or until boiling. Stir once and microwave on MEDIUM (50%) for 5 minutes longer or until rehydrated and bubbly. This will make approximately 3-4 servings.

From-Scratch Soups Versus "Open and Go"

From-scratch microwave soups take almost as long to cook as conventionally prepared soups. We have included several from-scratch microwave soups for you to try. You will have to decide if you want your microwave running for 1-2 hours.

A food processor or blender will make your life easier. All vegetables can be cut by hand, but a food processor speeds up the procedure and yields uniform shapes and sizes for even cooking. Soups are sometimes puréed for a smoother texture and food processors come in handy for these as well. If you don't have a processor available, you can push cooked veggies through a sieve or use a manual food mill.

Many recipes in this and other chapters call for vegetable broth or stock. We suggest you keep cans or aseptic boxes of broth on hand. Several companies, including Imagine Foods and Swanson Soups make several sizes of vegetable broth and stock. We've included a conventional recipe for vegetable stock on page 177. You can prepare this stock and freeze it for later use with microwave recipes.

Whether you cook from-scratch soups in the microwave or on the stove, you may want a faster way to soak beans. If you would like to microwave-soak your beans and legumes, follow the steps listed below.

Microwave-Soaking Dried Beans and Legumes
1. Rinse beans or legumes in cold water in a colander or strainer. Combine in a large microwave-safe bowl, covered with vented plastic wrap, and microwave on HIGH until the water has boiled using:
     a. 1 cup dried beans and 3 cups cold water for 7 minutes *or*
     b. 2 cups dried beans and 6 cups cold water for 12 minutes

2. Once the water has boiled, cook on MEDIUM (50%) for 2 minutes. Allow beans to stand, covered, for 45 minutes.

3. Discard any beans that are floating. Feel the beans; they should be tough, but a little soft. If they are still very hard, allow beans to soak for several more minutes.

4. Drain and rinse. Cook in fresh water.

Note: Some people believe that if you soak beans and cook in fresh water, you'll reduce the occurrence of flatulence. Other people like to cook with the water that beans have soaked in, believing that it gives extra flavor to dishes.

Vegetable Stock
(Makes 1 gallon)

If you can't find vegetable stock to buy or prefer to prepare your own, here's a conventional recipe for you to make in a large quantity and freeze in small quantities. In a freezer that is running properly, this stock will last up to 3 months.

1 Tablespoon vegetable oil
2 cloves garlic, chopped
2 Tablespoons chopped onion
1 gallon water (4 pints or 2 quarts or 16 cups)
3/4 cup dry white wine (optional)
1/2 cup minced carrots
1 cup sliced fresh mushrooms
3/4 cup minced celery
1/2 cup sliced leeks (or yellow onions)
Sachet (made with cheesecloth or a coffee filter) containing:
2 bay leaves
10 parsley stems
2 teaspoon whole black peppercorns
1 whole clove
1 teaspoon dried thyme

Add oil to a 1-1/2-gallon pot and heat. Add garlic and onion, and sauté until they are translucent (about 3 minutes). Add all remaining ingredients and bring to a fast boil. Lower heat, cover, and allow stock to simmer for 1 hour. Strain, cool properly, and refrigerate or freeze until needed.

Total Calories Per Serving Without Wine: 13   Total Fat as % of Daily Value: 1%
Protein: <1 gm   Fat: 1 gm   Carbohydrates: 1 gm   Calcium: 11 mg
Iron: <1 mg   Sodium: 14 mg   Dietary Fiber: <1 gm

Cream of Cauliflower
(Serves 6)

This soup is creamy and has a nice, spicy aftertaste.

1 Tablespoon oil
3/4 cup chopped onion
1/2 cup carrots, peeled and chopped
1-1/2 pounds cauliflower, chopped (3-1/2 cups)
4 cups vegetable broth or water
1 teaspoon white pepper
1/4 teaspoon cumin
1/4 teaspoon nutmeg
1 Tablespoon chopped fresh dill
1-1/2 cups soymilk

Combine oil and onion in a 3-quart casserole or bowl. Microwave on HIGH for 3 minutes or until the onion is tender. Add carrots, cauliflower, broth, white pepper, cumin, nutmeg, and dill, then stir to combine.

Cover with vented plastic or a lid and microwave on HIGH for 20 minutes or until vegetables are tender. Add soup by batches into the canister of a food processor or blender. Process until puréed and smooth. Return to casserole or bowl, cover, and microwave on HIGH for 2 minutes or until soup is warm.

Notes: Fresh broccoli, broccolini, or broccoli rabe can be used in place of the cauliflower. This soup does freeze well; however, it will be a little thinner when thawed.

Total Calories Per Serving: 88   Total Fat as % of Daily Value: 6%
Protein: 4 gm   Fat: 4 gm   Carbohydrates: 11 gm   Calcium: 24 mg
Iron: 1 mg   Sodium: 336 mg   Dietary Fiber: 3 gm

Potage Crecy
(Serves 6)

Here's a classic French soup that's colorful and "creamy" without the cream. This soup freezes well.

1 clove garlic, minced
1-1/2 cups chopped onion
2 Tablespoons oil
1/4 cup chopped celery
1 pound carrots, chopped (about 3-1/2 cups)
1/2 cup peeled and chopped boiling potatoes
4 cups vegetable stock or broth
1 teaspoon dried thyme
1/2 teaspoon dried dill
1 teaspoon white pepper
1/2 cup silken tofu

Combine garlic, onion, and oil in a 3-quart bowl or casserole and microwave on HIGH for 3 minutes or until the onions are tender. Add remaining ingredients, except tofu, and cover with vented plastic or a lid. Microwave on HIGH for 20 minutes or until the vegetables are tender.

Add soup to the canister of a food processor or blender and purée. Return to the bowl and stir in tofu. Cover and microwave on HIGH for 2 minutes or until soup is hot.

Note: Winter squash, such as Hubbard, acorn, turnips, or sweet potatoes can be used instead of carrots in this soup.

Total Calories Per Serving: 133   Total Fat as % of Daily Value: 8%
Protein: 3 gm   Fat: 5 gm   Carbohydrates: 19 gm   Calcium: 47 mg
Iron: 1 mg   Sodium: 341 mg   Dietary Fiber: 4 gm

Broccoli and Cheese Soup
(Serves 6)

Paired with cornbread and fruit salad, this soup make a terrific entrée.

1/2 cup chopped onion
1 Tablespoon oil
4 cups fresh broccoli, trimmed and chopped (whole
  stalk including the floret and stem)
3 cups vegetable stock
1 teaspoon white pepper
1 teaspoon dried parsley
2 Tablespoons flour
1 Tablespoon oil
1 cup silken tofu
1 cup grated vegan cheese

Combine onion with 1 Tablespoon oil in a 3-quart micro-wave-safe bowl or casserole and microwave on HIGH for 3 minutes or until onion is tender. Add broccoli, stock, pepper, and parsley and stir to combine. Cover with vented plastic or a lid and microwave on HIGH for 20 minutes or until broccoli is very tender. Remove and set aside.

In a 3-cup bowl or casserole, combine flour and oil and microwave on HIGH for 30 seconds or until bubbly. Stir to form a smooth paste. Gradually stir in tofu. Return to microwave and heat on HIGH for 2 minutes or until thickened. Remove from microwave, stir, then slowly add cheese, stirring until smooth. Set aside.

Add broccoli to food processor or blender canister and process until puréed.

Combine broccoli mixture and cheese mixture and stir to blend. Cover and microwave on HIGH for 2 minutes or until soup is hot.

Note: This soup freezes well. When reheating the soup, use MEDIUM; you don't want to toughen the cheese or overcook the broccoli.

Total Calories Per Serving: 157 Total Fat as % of Daily Value: 12%
Protein: 5 gm   Fat: 8 gm   Carbohydrates: 17 gm   Calcium: 46 mg
Iron: 1 mg   Sodium: 397 mg   Dietary Fiber: 2 gm

Fresh Summer Squash Soup
(Serves 5)

This soup has a delicate flavor and a wonderful aroma.

1-1/2 pounds fresh yellow squash or zucchini
(about 4 cups), washed and ends trimmed off
2 cups vegetable broth or stock
1/4 cup chopped onions
1 clove garlic, minced
2 Tablespoon chopped fresh parsley or cilantro
1/2 teaspoon thyme
1 teaspoon white pepper
1/4 cup chopped, cooked vegan fake meat such as
Tofurky, veggie hot dogs or sausage, Field Roast,
etc. (optional)

Cut squash into small cubes or chunks. In a 2-quart casserole or bowl, combine all ingredients, stirring to mix. Cover with vented plastic or a lid and microwave on HIGH for 12 minutes or until vegetables are tender. Stir at least twice during cooking. Place 2 cups of the soup in a blender or food processor and process until smooth. Return to remaining soup and stir to combine. Microwave on HIGH for 2 minutes or until hot.

Note: This soup works well with any soft-shelled squash, such as crookneck, delicata, and patty pan. You can mix several squashes in one batch, if desired. Do not prepare this soup with frozen or canned squash.

Total Calories Per Serving Without "Meat": 33
Total Fat as % of Daily Value: 0%
Protein: 2 gm   Fat: <1 gm   Carbohydrates: 7 gm   Calcium: 22 mg
Iron: 1 mg   Sodium: 188 mg   Dietary Fiber: 2 gm

Fast Barley Soup
(Serves 5)

No one will know you didn't make this soup from scratch!

4 cups vegetable stock
3/4 cup quick-cooking barley
1 cup sliced canned mushrooms, drained
1 teaspoon white pepper

Place stock in a 2-quart container or casserole and micro-wave on HIGH for 5-6 minutes to bring it to a boil (the boiling time depends on your microwave). Mix in barley and microwave on HIGH for 4 minutes or until the barley is tender. Mix in mushrooms and pepper and microwave for 1 minute longer on HIGH. Remove from microwave, stir, and let stand covered for 5 minutes to allow the flavors to blend. Serve hot.

Total Calories Per Serving: 113   Total Fat as % of Daily Value: 0%
Protein: 4 gm   Fat: 1 gm   Carbohydrates: 23 gm   Calcium: 7 mg
Iron: 1 mg   Sodium: 546 mg   Dietary Fiber: 3 gm

Creamy Pumpkin Soup

(Serves 3)

Save the shell of a pumpkin or a hard squash in which to
serve this soup.

2 teaspoons oil
1/2 cup chopped onion
2 cups vegetable broth
2 cups canned pumpkin purée (not seasoned or
   sweetened)
1-1/2 cups soymilk
1/2 teaspoon garlic powder
1/2 teaspoon onion powder
1 teaspoon dried parsley

Toss oil and onion together in a 2-quart bowl or casserole.
Microwave on HIGH for 4 minutes or until onion is tender.
Add broth and pumpkin. Cover and microwave on HIGH
for 12 minutes. Stir. Add in milk and seasonings and stir.
Microwave on HIGH for 3 minutes or until soup is
thoroughly heated.

Note: This recipe can be used to make a creamy tomato
soup using 2 cups tomato purée instead of pumpkin, or
for a creamy potato soup use 2 cups thin mashed potatoes
(you can thin prepared mashed potatoes with water or
milk) instead of the pumpkin.

Total Calories Per Serving: 156   Total Fat as % of Daily Value: 9%
Protein: 6 gm   Fat: 6 gm   Carbohydrates: 22 gm   Calcium: 57 mg
Iron: 3 mg   Sodium: 331 mg   Dietary Fiber: 7 gm

Red Pepper Soup
(Serves 4)

This soup keeps you warm for hours.

1 Tablespoon vegan margarine
2 cloves garlic, minced
1/4 cup chopped green onions
2 pounds fresh red bell peppers, seeded and cut
    into chunks (about 4-1/4 cups)
3 cups vegetable stock
1/8 teaspoon hot sauce
1/8 teaspoon cayenne pepper

Put margarine in a 2-quart bowl or measure and microwave on HIGH for 20-30 seconds or until melted. Add garlic, onion, and peppers. Microwave on HIGH for 6 minutes until the peppers are crisp, but tender. Add stock, hot sauce, and cayenne pepper. Cover and microwave on HIGH for 12 minutes until the peppers are tender. Place in a food processor or blender and purée. Return soup to the bowl, taste, and add more seasoning, if desired (remember, the "heat" will intensify in about 10 minutes). Microwave on HIGH for 2 minutes or until thoroughly heated.

Total Calories Per Serving: 98   Total Fat as % of Daily Value: 5%
Protein: 2 gm   Fat: 3 gm   Carbohydrates: 16 gm   Calcium: 19 mg
Iron: 1 mg   Sodium: 384 mg   Dietary Fiber: 4 gm

Russian Beet Borscht
(Serves 9)

This soup is deep crimson in color and rich in flavor. It can be served cold or hot.

2 pounds fresh beets, greens removed and peeled
1 whole onion (about 8 ounces or 1 cup)
6 cups hot water
2-1/2 cups tomato juice
1/2 cup vegan dry sweetener
2 Tablespoons lemon juice
2 teaspoons chopped fresh dill

Grate beets and onions until coarse. Save the juice.

Combine grated beets and onions and their juice with all the remaining ingredients in a 3-quart casserole or bowl. Cover with vented plastic or a lid. Microwave on HIGH for 40 minutes or until the beets have become tender. Let stand covered for 10 minutes. Taste to see if you need more lemon or sweetener, depending on your preference. Allow soup to chill in the refrigerator for at least 1 hour before serving.

Notes: Beets stain your hands and your kitchen. You may want to peel the beets outside or while wearing rubber gloves. The beet greens can be saved and finely shredded and added raw to salads or cooked vegetable dishes. Or you could chop the greens and steam them, covered, for 10 minutes on HIGH for a side dish.

Traditionally, borscht is garnished with boiled potatoes and a small amount of sour cream (you can use vegan sour cream). You may freeze this borscht and allow it to thaw when ready to use.

Total Calories Per Serving: 103   Total Fat as % of Daily Value: 0%
Protein: 2 gm   Fat: <1 gm   Carbohydrates: 24 gm   Calcium: 37 mg
Iron: 1 mg   Sodium: 327 mg   Dietary Fiber: 3 gm

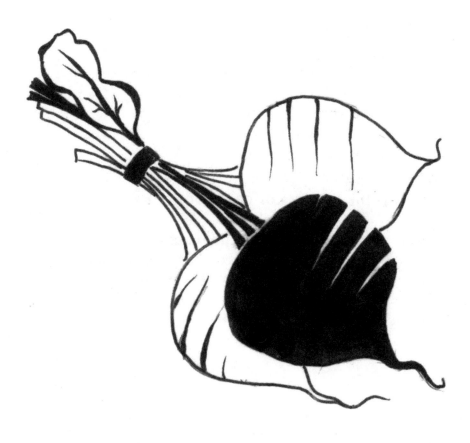

Potato and Asparagus Vichyssoise (Cold Potato and Asparagus Soup)
(Serves 6)

This soup was invented in New York City by a homesick chef from Vichy.

1 pound fresh asparagus, stemmed and peeled (or
    1 pound frozen asparagus, thawed)
2 cloves garlic, minced
1/2 cup chopped onion
2 Tablespoons oil
3/4 cup chopped carrots
2 cups peeled and chopped boiling potatoes
1 teaspoon black pepper
1/2 teaspoon dried tarragon
1 teaspoon dried parsley
1/2 teaspoon onion powder
4 cups hot water
1 cup soymilk or soy coffee creamer

Cut asparagus in 1-inch pieces and set aside. Combine garlic, onion, and oil in 3-quart bowl or casserole and microwave on HIGH for 3 minutes or until onions are tender.

Add carrots, potatoes, pepper, tarragon, parsley, onion powder, and water. Cover with vented plastic or a lid and microwave on HIGH for 20 minutes or until vegetables are fork-tender (easily mashed with a fork).

Place soup in a food processor or blender and process until smooth. Add milk and stir until combined. Chill for at least one hour before serving.

Notes: Fresh asparagus should be peeled (you can use a vegetable peeler) so that the tough outer skin of the asparagus does not make the soup chewy. If a blender or food processor is not available, you can purée the soup by pushing it through a strainer.

West Soy sells "Crème de le Soy," a soy coffee creamer. You can use the unflavored or plain version to make a creamy soup. If this is not available, you can use soymilk for a thin version or silken tofu for a thicker version.

Total Calories Per Serving: 128   Total Fat as % of Daily Value: 8%
Protein: 4 gm   Fat: 5 gm   Carbohydrates: 16 gm   Calcium: 38 mg
Iron: 1 mg   Sodium: 19 mg   Dietary Fiber: 4 gm

Cucumber and Avocado Soup

(Serves 6)

Serve this cold soup on a warm summer's night.

1-1/2 cups chopped onions
1 Tablespoon oil
2 cucumbers, peeled, seeded, and diced (about
   2 cups)
2 Tablespoons minced fresh parsley
2 cloves garlic, minced
4 cups vegetable stock or broth
1 teaspoon black pepper
1/2 teaspoon dried oregano
1/4 teaspoon Tabasco or hot sauce
3 very ripe avocados, peeled and pitted (about
   1-1/2 cups)

In a 2-quart bowl or casserole, combine onion and oil.
Microwave on HIGH for 3 minutes, stirring once. Add
cucumbers, parsley, and garlic. Cover with vented plastic or
a lid. Microwave on HIGH for 3 minutes or until cucumbers
are soft. Add stock, pepper, oregano, and Tabasco. Cover
and microwave on HIGH for 12 minutes. Allow mixture to
stand for 5 minutes to cool, then strain, saving juice.

Place cucumber solids and avocado in a food processor
or blender and process until smooth. Combine cucumber
liquid and avocado mixture together and stir until smooth.
Allow soup to chill for at least one hour before serving.

Total Calories Per Serving: 225   Total Fat as % of Daily Value: 27%
Protein: 4 gm   Fat: 18 gm   Carbohydrates: 17 gm   Calcium: 32 mg
Iron: 1 mg   Sodium: 321 mg   Dietary Fiber: 6 gm

Avocado Dip (Guacamole)
(Makes about 2-1/2 cups)

You'll find a twist here on the traditional recipe for guacamole.

2 cloves garlic, minced
1/2 cup chopped onion
1 teaspoon oil
2 avocados, pitted and peeled (about 1-1/2 cups)
1/2 cup chopped red bell pepper
1 Tablespoon chopped cilantro (optional)
2 Tablespoons vegan mayonnaise
2 Tablespoons lime juice
1/4 cup vegan sour cream or vegan unflavored
  yogurt
1 teaspoon red pepper flakes or Tabasco sauce

Mix garlic, onion, and oil in a small bowl and microwave on HIGH for 2 minutes or until tender.

In a large bowl, mash avocados. Add garlic mixture and remaining ingredients and mix and mash until well combined. Refrigerate in a plastic or glass container, covered. Chill for at least one hour before serving.

Note: If the avocados aren't soft enough to mash, you can microwave them on HIGH for 1 minute.

Total Calories Per Serving Using Sour Cream: 50
Total Fat as % of Daily Value: 7%
Protein: 1 gm   Fat: 4 gm   Carbohydrates: 3 gm   Calcium: 4 mg
Iron: <1 mg   Sodium: 21 mg   Dietary Fiber: 1 gm

Baba Ganouyh
(Garlic-Eggplant Dip)
(Makes about 2 cups or 8 servings)

This Middle Eastern dish can be used as a spread for sandwiches, a dip for veggies or chips, or as a topping for rice, pasta, couscous, or roasted or steamed veggies.

1-1/4 pounds eggplant (1 large)
3 cloves garlic, minced
1/4 cup minced onion
3 Tablespoons vegan mayonnaise
3 Tablespoons lemon juice
2 Tablespoons chopped green onions
1 Tablespoon sliced black olives (for garnish)

Wash eggplant and dry well. Pierce in several places with a fork. Place eggplant on a microwave-safe rack. Microwave on HIGH, calculating 5 minutes per pound of eggplant. A 1-1/4 pound eggplant should microwave in 7 minutes. Halfway through cooking, turn eggplant over. Allow it to cook until it is very tender when pieced with a fork. You want the eggplant to cook into pulp. Remember that it will continue to cook as it stands, so you don't want it to become extremely soft in the microwave.

Remove eggplant from the microwave and allow to cool for 10 minutes. When eggplant is cool, cut it in half and scoop out the pulp.

In the canister of a food processor or blender, place the eggplant pulp and the remaining ingredients (except the black olive garnish). Process until smooth. This can also be done by hand, in a mixing bowl.

Spread baba ganoujh on a serving plate and garnish with black olives before serving.

Total Calories Per Serving: 49   Total Fat as % of Daily Value: 4%
Protein: 1 gm   Fat: 3 gm   Carbohydrates: 7 gm   Calcium: 8 mg
Iron: <1 mg   Sodium: 21 mg   Dietary Fiber: 2 gm

Tzatziki
(Greek Cucumber Dip)
(Makes 1-1/2 cups sauce or 6 servings)

You don't need a microwave to prepare this dip. Use it over microwave-cooked vegetables and potatoes.

2 cloves garlic, minced
2 Tablespoon minced fresh dill
1 cup peeled, deseeded, and grated cucumber
1 teaspoon white pepper
1/2 cup vegan mayonnaise
1/2 cup vegan sour cream or vegan unflavored
    yogurt

In a medium-size mixing bowl, combine garlic and dill. Squeeze any liquid out from cucumber. Add cucumber, pepper, mayonnaise, and sour cream or yogurt to bowl and mix well. Chill for at least one hour before serving.

Note: To deseed the cucumber, cut cucumber in half, lengthwise, and scoop out seeds.

Total Calories Per Serving Using Sour Cream: 129
Total Fat as % of Daily Value: 19%
Protein: 1 gm   Fat: 12 gm   Carbohydrates: 5 gm   Calcium: 6 mg
Iron: <1 mg   Sodium: 147 mg   Dietary Fiber: <1 gm

193

Capanata
(Makes about 2-1/2 cups or 10 servings)

Use capanata as a dip for vegetables and breads and crackers or as an ingredient in soups and casseroles.

1-1/2 pounds eggplant (about 3-1/2 cups)
2 cloves garlic, minced
3/4 cup chopped onions
1/4 cup celery, minced
3 Tablespoons olive oil (divided into 1 Tablespoon
    and 2 Tablespoons)
2 cups prepared tomato sauce
3 Tablespoons tomato paste
2 Tablespoons vinegar
1/4 cup raisins
1 Tablespoon dry vegan sweetener
1/2 cup sliced green olives
1/2 cup sliced black olives

Cut eggplant (do not peel) into small chunks. Cover with a paper towel and set aside. Place garlic, onion, celery, and 1 Tablespoon oil in a 2-cup bowl or measure. Microwave on HIGH for 5 minutes or until onions are tender. Set aside. Combine eggplant and 2 Tablespoons olive oil and toss to coat eggplant. Place mixture in a medium-size bowl and microwave on HIGH for 6 minutes or until eggplant is tender.

Drain eggplant and discard liquid. Add sauce, paste, vinegar, raisins, and sweetener and mix. Microwave covered on HIGH for 10 minutes or until mixture is very tender. Let stand, covered, for 5 minutes to cool. Mix in olives. Serve hot or cold.

Total Calories Per Serving: 112   Total Fat as % of Daily Value: 9%
Protein: 2 gm   Fat: 6 gm   Carbohydrates: 15 gm   Calcium: 24 mg
Iron: 1 mg   Sodium: 479 mg   Dietary Fiber: 3 gm

Spinach and Parsley Salad Dressing

(Makes about 2 cups or 20 one-ounce servings)

This dip is often served in a hollowed-out, round loaf of sourdough bread.

10-ounce package frozen chopped spinach
1/4 cup chopped onion
1/2 cup chopped fresh parsley
1 cup vegan sour cream or vegan unflavored yogurt
1 teaspoon black pepper

Cut spinach package in several places with a knife or scissors. Place on a microwave-safe plate. Microwave on HIGH for 4 minutes or until completely thawed. Remove from microwave, unwrap, and allow to cool. Squeeze extremely dry and discard liquid.

Place spinach, parsley, sour cream or yogurt, and pepper in a medium bowl and mix until well combined. If a very smooth texture is desired, you can mix this in a blender or food processor.

Allow to chill for at least two hours before serving.

Note: If vegan sour cream or yogurt are not available, you can use 1 cup of silken tofu blended with 2 teaspoons lemon juice.

Total Calories Per Serving Using Sour Cream: 24
Total Fat as % of Daily Value: 3%
Protein: 1 gm   Fat: 2 gm   Carbohydrates: 1 gm   Calcium: 18 mg
Iron: <1 mg   Sodium: 58 mg   Dietary Fiber: 1 gm

Tri-Color Herbed Peppers

(Makes 4 servings as a side dish or dip.
If puréed, makes about 1-1/2 cups sauce.)

Serve this mixture as a side dish, sauce, or condiment.

2 teaspoons olive oil
1 medium red bell pepper, seeded and cut into thin slices (about 3/4 cup)
1 medium orange or yellow bell pepper, seeded and cut into thin slices (about 3/4 cup)
1 medium green bell pepper, seeded and cut into thin slices (about 3/4 cup)
1 clove garlic, minced
1 Tablespoon balsamic vinegar or red sherry
1 Tablespoon minced fresh basil
1 teaspoon dried oregano
1 teaspoon dried sage
1 teaspoon black pepper

In a 2-quart bowl or casserole, toss oil, peppers, and garlic. Microwave on HIGH for 2 minutes or until peppers are tender. Add remaining ingredients, cover, and microwave on HIGH for 1 minute. Stir (to combine flavors) and serve.

Notes: If a smooth sauce is desired, microwave the cooked peppers for an additional 1-1/2 minutes. Place in a food processor or blender and process until puréed. Serve warm over cooked vegetables or pasta, or as a sauce for baked tofu or a seitan "steak." Serve cold as a dipping sauce for veggies, chips, or breadsticks, or use as a salad dressing.

Total Calories Per Serving Using Vinegar: 51   Total Fat as % of Daily Value: 4%
Protein: 1 gm   Fat: 2 gm   Carbohydrates: 7 gm   Calcium: 22 mg
Iron: 1 mg   Sodium: 3 mg   Dietary Fiber: 2 gm

CHAPTER EIGHT
Microwave Breakfast and Hot Beverages

The microwave must have been designed with morning in mind. In a matter of minutes you can have a steaming hot beverage, warm bread, and a cinnamony bowl of oatmeal. You don't ever have to expose your morning-fogged brain to an open flame (unless, of course, you leave a metal spoon in your coffee cup as you microwave it!).

If you're in a rush, against cooking in the morning, or your cooking equipment consists of a microwave only, then you're in luck. You can brew your coffee right off the bat. Then you can decide on a hot bowl of cereal, a warm muffin, or a fruit cobbler for breakfast.

Some A.M. Microwave Tips
• One square of matzo or flat bread can get crisp and toasty when microwaved on HIGH for 30 seconds. Instead of toast, have a crispy piece of matzo or flatbread with nut butters and fruit preserves for breakfast.
• Overheating makes bread, rolls, and pastry tough. If you would like to reheat a roll or a pastry, wrap it in several thicknesses of paper towels or a clean cloth towel. Start with 20 seconds on MEDIUM HIGH. If the item still is not as hot as you'd like, heat further in 20-second intervals to avoid toughness.

• Jelly gets very hot in the microwave—hot enough to scorch your fingers and the inside of your mouth. Heat jelly-containing pastries or bread and jelly just until warm to avoid rude and dangerous awakenings.

• Soft tofu quickly mixed with a small amount of apple juice concentrate and maple syrup then microwaved until hot makes a warm, get-up-and-go breakfast on chilly mornings.

• Veggie bacon or sausage can be microwaved and eaten on toast with sliced tomatoes or scrambled tofu.

• Frozen edamame (soybeans) can be microwaved in under 2 minutes. Paired with a soy smoothie, they make a high protein, crunchy breakfast.

• If savory is your A.M. thing, then alternate slices of firm tofu and tomatoes on a small plate and microwave until hot. You can prepare this dish the night before. Just grab it from the refrigerator when you're ready to heat it.

• "Souffles" of a sort can be made in the microwave. We've included two recipes for these, one corn and one matzo-based. They will fluff up in the microwave, but will lose their heads fairly quickly. Prepare them and eat them right away.

• No one says you can't have a baked potato for breakfast. Microwave an extra white or sweet potato the night before and reheat it in the microwave the next morning.

• Many cold cereals taste very good when they're warmed up. We've tried raisin and bran flake and Grapenut™-type cereals with good results. Pour the amount of cereal you would like into a microwave-safe bowl, add just enough milk to moisten, mix around a bit, and microwave until warm.

Oatmeal for One
(Serves 1)

This hot cereal is so easy!

1/4 cup quick (1-minute) rolled oats
1/2 cup water
1/8 teaspoon salt (optional)

Pour oatmeal into a small bowl. Stir in water and salt.
Microwave on HIGH for 1 minute 10 seconds or until thick.
Remove from microwave, stir, cover, and let stand for
2 minutes before eating.

Total Calories Per Serving: 73   Total Fat as % of Daily Value: 2%
Protein: 3 gm   Fat: 1 gm   Carbohydrates: 13 gm   Calcium: 13 mg
Iron: 1 mg   Sodium: 4 mg   Dietary Fiber: 2 gm

Oatmeal for the Whole Crew
(Serves 4)

Let everyone start the day right with this simple cereal.

1-1/2 cups quick (1-minute) rolled oats
3 cups water
1 teaspoon salt (optional)

Pour oatmeal in a 2-quart casserole or bowl. Stir in water
and salt. Microwave on HIGH for 6-8 minutes or until thick.
Remove from microwave, stir, cover, and let stand for
4 minutes before eating.

Total Calories Per Serving: 110   Total Fat as % of Daily Value: 3%
Protein: 4 gm   Fat: 2 gm   Carbohydrates: 20 gm   Calcium: 19 mg
Iron: 1 mg   Sodium: 6 mg   Dietary Fiber: 3 gm

Hot Cornmeal Cereal
(Serves 5)

Leftovers can be baked in the oven with a little bit of tomato sauce for a quick lunch!

1 cup yellow cornmeal
4 cups water
2 teaspoons salt (optional)

Pour cornmeal into a 2-quart casserole. Stir in water and salt. Microwave on HIGH for 10 minutes. Remove from microwave, stir, and let stand 5 minutes before eating.

Total Calories Per Serving: 88   Total Fat as % of Daily Value: 1%
Protein: 2 gm   Fat: 1 gm   Carbohydrates: 19 gm   Calcium: 5 mg
Iron: 1 mg   Sodium: 14 mg   Dietary Fiber: 2 gm

Hominy Grits
(Serves 4)

These grits are fast and easy. Leftovers can be used to thicken sauces and soup.

1 cup hominy grits (not instant)
3-3/4 cups water

Combine grits and water in a 3-quart bowl or casserole. Cover and microwave on HIGH for 5 minutes. Stir well. Cover and microwave on HIGH for 5 more minutes or until all the liquid is absorbed. Let stand for 2 minutes. Stir and serve.

Note: For 1 serving, use 1/4 cup grits and 1 cup water, microwaving only once for 4 minutes.

Total Calories Per Serving: 142 Total Fat as % of Daily Value: 1%
Protein: 4 gm   Fat: 1 gm   Carbohydrates: 32 gm   Calcium: 6 mg
Iron: 1 mg   Sodium: 7 mg   Dietary Fiber: 2 gm

Cornmeal Mini-Soufflés
(Makes 4)

If you used this same mixture on a heated grill, it would make cornmeal pancakes. In the microwave it will puff up and have a fluffy texture. These are a good source of iron and calcium.

1 cup cake flour (flour that has been extra ground)
1 cup yellow cornmeal
1 Tablespoon baking powder
1 teaspoon salt
3 Tablespoons vegan dry sweetener
1/2 cup silken tofu
1 cup soy or rice milk
Vegetable oil spray

Sift together flour, cornmeal, baking powder, salt, and sweetener in a medium-size bowl. Whip tofu until it is light and fluffy (you can do this in a blender or with a mixer).

   The next steps must be done quickly to capture the air you've whipped into the tofu. Quickly fold the tofu into the dry ingredients. Quickly mix in the milk. Spray 4 custard cups with vegetable oil. Quickly pour the mixture into the cups. Arrange on a microwave turntable and microwave on HIGH for 3 minutes or until you see the soufflés rise and form a crust (the crust will not be brown). Serve.

Total Calories Per Serving: 308 Total Fat as % of Daily Value: 5%
Protein: 8 gm   Fat: 3 gm   Carbohydrates: 62 gm   Calcium: 230 mg
Iron: 5 mg   Sodium: 971 mg   Dietary Fiber: 4 gm

Matzo Meal Mini-Soufflés
(Makes 4)

This dish is not quite as delicate as a traditional soufflé, but fluffy and wonderful for breakfast.

1/2 cup matzo meal
1 teaspoon salt
1 Tablespoon vegan dry sweetener
1/2 cup silken tofu
1 cup soy or rice milk

Combine matzo meal, salt, and sweetener in a medium bowl. Whip tofu with a blender or mixer until it is light and fluffy.

The next steps must be done quickly to get the "puff" of the soufflé. Fold the tofu into the dry ingredients. Quickly stir in the milk. Spray 4 custard cups with vegetable oil. Quickly pour the mixture into the cups and microwave on HIGH for 3 minutes or until the soufflés rise and a crust is formed (the crust will not be brown). Serve.

Total Calories Per Serving: 87   Total Fat as % of Daily Value: 3%
Protein: 4 gm   Fat: 2 gm   Carbohydrates: 13 gm   Calcium: 17 mg
Iron: 1 mg   Sodium: 592 mg   Dietary Fiber: 1 gm

French Toast Matzo
(Serves 4)

Bread does not get crispy enough in the microwave, but matzo and other flatbreads do.

2/3 cup silken tofu
1/2 teaspoon vanilla extract
1/4 teaspoon lemon zest
4 matzo
2 teaspoons vegan dry sweetener
2 teaspoons ground cinnamon
Vegetable oil spray

Whip tofu, vanilla, and zest in a medium-size bowl with a blender or mixer until fluffy. Pour mixture onto a dinner plate or shallow pan. Dip each piece of matzo into the tofu mixture and sprinkle with sweetener and cinnamon.

Spray a microwave-safe dinner plate or shallow pan with vegetable oil. Place one matzo on the plate and microwave on HIGH for 1 minute. Turn over and microwave for 2 minutes. Repeat with the remaining matzo. Serve hot, with maple syrup and fruit preserves.

Total Calories Per Serving: 147
Protein: 5 gm   Fat: 2 gm
Iron: 1 mg   Sodium: 4 mg
Total Fat as % of Daily Value: 2%
Carbohydrates: 28 gm   Calcium: 29 mg
Dietary Fiber: 1 gm

Rice for Breakfast
(Serves 5)

Use leftovers for lunch in burritos, casseroles, and soups.

2-1/2 cups water
1 cup long grain white rice
1 teaspoon salt (optional)

Pour water into a 2-quart casserole or bowl and microwave on HIGH for 3-4 minutes or until boiling. Stir in rice and salt. Cover with a lid or vented plastic. Microwave on HIGH for 6-7 minutes or until all water is absorbed. Remove from the microwave and let dish stand covered for 10 minutes. Fluff with a fork before serving.

Total Calories Per Serving: 135   Total Fat as % of Daily Value: 0%
Protein: 3 gm   Fat: <1 gm   Carbohydrates: 30 gm   Calcium: 13 mg
Iron: <1 mg   Sodium: 5 mg   Dietary Fiber: <1 gm

Blueberry Sauce
(Makes about 2 cups or 8 servings)

Serve with hot cereal, or over steamed tofu or hot rice, along with cooked fruit or fresh muffins.

2 cups fresh or frozen, thawed blueberries
1/2 cup vegan dry sweetener
2 Tablespoons orange juice
1/2 cup water
2 Tablespoons cornstarch
1/4 cup water

In a 2-quart bowl or measure, combine blueberries, sweetener, orange juice, and 1/2 cup water. Microwave on HIGH for 4 minutes or until bubbling.

In a small cup or bowl, combine cornstarch and 1/4 cup water. Stir until smooth. Stir cornstarch into blueberries. Microwave on HIGH for 2-3 minutes longer, until sauce is thickened. If the sauce becomes too thick, stir in a small amount of water or orange juice.

Total Calories Per Serving: 75   Total Fat as % of Daily Value: 0%
Protein: <1 gm   Fat: <1 gm   Carbohydrates: 19 gm   Calcium: 13 mg
Iron: <1 mg   Sodium: 8 mg   Dietary Fiber: 1 gm

Hot Applesauce
(Serves 6)

Serve this over steamed tofu, hot cereal, or with muffins.

6-7 medium-sized baking apples, peeled and cored
   (about 6 cups or 3 pounds)
1/4 cup apple juice
3 Tablespoons vegan dry sweetener
2 teaspoons cinnamon
1 teaspoon ground ginger
1 teaspoon lemon juice

Cut apples in large pieces and put in a 2-quart measure or casserole. Add remaining ingredients and toss. Cover and microwave on HIGH for 6-8 minutes or until apples are tender. You can gently mash apples for a smoother sauce or serve this chunky-style.

Note: This recipe can be frozen. Try to use baking apples, such as Romes, MacIntosh, Cortlands, or Jonathans.

Total Calories Per Serving: 94   Total Fat as % of Daily Value: 0%
Protein: <1 gm   Fat: <1 gm   Carbohydrates: 24 gm   Calcium: 17 mg
Iron: <1 mg   Sodium: 3 mg   Dietary Fiber: 3 gm

Rhubarb Sauce
(Makes 2 cups or 8 servings)

This sauce is a little tangy and a little sweet. Serve it with steamed tofu, cooked fruit, or pastries.

1-1/2 cups sliced fresh or frozen, thawed rhubarb
1/2 cup vegan sweetener
2 Tablespoons apple juice concentrate
1/2 cup water

Place all ingredients in a microwave-safe 1-quart bowl. Cover and microwave on HIGH for 4 minutes or until rhubarb is very tender. Remove and stir sauce until smooth. Serve with hot cereals, pancakes, waffles, and hot muffins.

Total Calories Per Serving: 58   Total Fat as % of Daily Value: 0%
Protein: <1 gm   Fat: <1 gm   Carbohydrates: 15 gm   Calcium: 31 mg
Iron: <1 mg   Sodium: 7 mg   Dietary Fiber: <1 gm

Dried Fruit Stew
(Serves 6)

This stew tastes great hot or cold; leftovers can be served with an entrée for dinner. The stew is a good source of iron.

1-1/2 pounds mixed dried fruit (about 3-1/4 cups)
1 cup raisins
1/2 cup sliced oranges
2 Tablespoons maple syrup
1 Tablespoon minced candied or dried ginger
3 cups apple or orange juice

Place all ingredients in a 2-quart bowl or casserole. Cover and microwave on HIGH for 12 minutes. Stir. Let stand 10 minutes before serving. Fruit will plump up as it stands.

Note: This dish tastes good hot or cold. It will keep in the refrigerator for up to a week.

Total Calories Per Serving: 429   Total Fat as % of Daily Value: 1%
Protein: 4 gm   Fat: 1 gm   Carbohydrates: 114 gm   Calcium: 66 mg
Iron: 4 mg   Sodium: 33 mg   Dietary Fiber: 11 gm

Stewed Fresh Rhubarb
(Serves 5)

Rhubarb is crimson and pink, slightly puckery, and slightly sweet. Serve this with sweetened cooked or cold cereal or with cooked fruit.

4 cups sliced rhubarb
1/4 cup orange juice
3/4 cup vegan dry sweetener
1 cup sliced strawberries, fresh or frozen, thawed

In a 2-quart bowl or casserole, combine rhubarb, juice, and sweetener. Cover and microwave on HIGH for 10 minutes or until rhubarb is tender. Stir in strawberries. Let stand at least 10 minutes before serving.

Note: Be sure that all the rhubarb leaves are removed before cooking. If rhubarb looks tough or old, it can be peeled with a potato peeler to remove the strings. More sweetener may be needed, depending on the rhubarb's tartness.

Total Calories Per Serving: 146   Total Fat as % of Daily Value: 0%
Protein: 1 gm   Fat: <1 gm   Carbohydrates: 37 gm   Calcium: 115 mg
Iron: 1 mg   Sodium: 16 mg   Dietary Fiber: 3 gm

Micro-Broiled Grapefruit
(Serves 2)

Take a break from juice and prepare this quick-and-easy breakfast.

1 large pink or red grapefruit, cut in half
4 teaspoons maple syrup

Place each grapefruit half on a plate. Segment with a knife, if desired. Drizzle 2 teaspoons of syrup over each half. If your microwave has room, microwave both halves at the same time, about 1-1/2 minutes on HIGH. Individually, each grapefruit half should take about 40-50 seconds.

Total Calories Per Serving: 72   Total Fat as % of Daily Value: 0%
Protein: 1 gm   Fat: <1 gm   Carbohydrates: 18 gm   Calcium: 23 mg
Iron: <1 mg   Sodium: 1 mg   Dietary Fiber: 2 gm

Citrus Dried Plums
(Serves 6)

Make a big batch of these and store in the refrigerator. This dish is a good source of iron and great for breakfast, to go with cooked grains, or with a scoop of sorbet for dessert.

1-1/2 pounds pitted dried prunes (about 3-1/4 cups)
1 cup raisins
3 cups water
1/4 cup vegan dry sweetener
1/4 cup diced, peeled fresh lemon
1/2 cup diced, peeled fresh orange

Place all the ingredients in a 2-quart casserole or bowl and combine. Cover and microwave on HIGH for 12 minutes. Stir and allow dish to stand for at least 10 minutes before serving.

Note: This dish will last for up to a week in the refrigerator.

Total Calories Per Serving: 369   Total Fat as % of Daily Value: 1%
Protein: 4 gm   Fat: 1 gm   Carbohydrates: 98 gm   Calcium: 82 mg
Iron: 4 mg   Sodium: 18 mg   Dietary Fiber: 11 gm

Spicy Dried Fruit Compote
(Serves 6)

What a way to get your vitamins and minerals! Stir the compote into soy yogurt or hot cereal, or eat it on its own.

1 cup dried plums (prunes)
1/2 cup dried mixed fruit
2 Tablespoons dry vegan sweetener
1/4 teaspoon ground allspice
1 teaspoon ground cinnamon
1/2 teaspoon ground ginger
2 cups water

In a 1-quart microwave-safe bowl, combine all ingredients and stir to mix. Cover and vent. Microwave on HIGH for 3 minutes or until boiling. Remove compote from the microwave and allow to cool for at least 30 minutes before serving.

Total Calories Per Serving: 113   Total Fat as % of Daily Value: 0%
Protein: 1 gm   Fat: <1 gm   Carbohydrates: 29 gm   Calcium: 28 mg
Iron: 1 mg   Sodium: 7 mg   Dietary Fiber: 3 gm

Gingery Figs
(Serves 6)

This luxurious side dish can stand alone for breakfast or be stirred into soy yogurt or hot cereal.

1 pound dried figs (about 2-1/4 cups)
2 Tablespoons lemon juice
2 teaspoons lemon zest
2 Tablespoons grated fresh ginger
2 Tablespoons maple syrup

Remove stems from figs, if necessary. Place in a large microwave-safe bowl and cover with cold water. Add lemon juice, zest, and ginger. Cover and microwave on HIGH for 4 minutes or until the figs have puffed up and are soft. Stir in maple syrup. Microwave on HIGH for 1 minute. Serve hot or cold.

Total Calories Per Serving: 234   Total Fat as % of Daily Value: 0%
Protein: 2 gm   Fat: <1 gm   Carbohydrates: 55 gm   Calcium: 107 mg
Iron: 2 mg   Sodium: 10 mg   Dietary Fiber: 9 gm

Hot Fruit Stew
(Serves 6)

Pair this stew with toast or a muffin for a full breakfast. Add a little rice or vanilla soymilk for a creamy note.

Vegetable oil spray
2 Tablespoons maple syrup
2 teaspoons orange zest
1 teaspoon cornstarch
1/3 cup orange juice
2 Tablespoons lemon juice

4 cups mixed fresh fruit, cut into small chunks,
    such as bananas, peaches, apricots, pears,
    oranges, pineapple, apples, or blueberries

Spray vegetable oil in a large microwave-safe bowl. Add remaining ingredients, except fruit. Microwave on HIGH for 2 minutes. Remove and stir briskly. If the sauce does not thicken after 2 minutes of stirring, return to the microwave and microwave on HIGH for 1 more minute. Gently stir in fruit. Cover and vent. Microwave on HIGH for 1 minute or just until the fruit is warm. Serve immediately.

Total Calories Per Serving: 82   Total Fat as % of Daily Value: 0%
Protein: 1 gm   Fat: <1 gm   Carbohydrates: 21 gm   Calcium: 15 mg
Iron: <1 mg   Sodium: 3 mg   Dietary Fiber: 2 gm

Baked Raisins and Apricots
(Serves 6)

Use leftovers as a pie filling or mix into stuffing or rice.

1/2 pound dried apricots (about 1 cup)
1 cup seedless raisins
2 cups water
1/2 cup vegan dry sweetener
2 Tablespoons lemon juice
1/2 cup chopped fresh orange (peeled)

Combine apricots and raisins in a large microwave-safe bowl. Add water, cover, and microwave on HIGH for 4 minutes. Stir in sweetener, lemon juice, and orange. Stir until sweetener is dissolved. Serve warm or cold.

Total Calories Per Serving: 242   Total Fat as % of Daily Value: 0%
Protein: 2 gm   Fat: <1 gm   Carbohydrates: 61 gm   Calcium: 47 mg
Iron: 2 mg   Sodium: 17 mg   Dietary Fiber: 4 gm

A.M. Poached Pears
(Serves 4)

The spices in this dish will give you an A.M. smile.

1 cup cranberry juice
1 teaspoon cinnamon
1 teaspoon lemon or orange zest
2 Tablespoons orange juice concentrate
4 ripe (but still firm) pears

In a 1-quart bowl or measure, combine juice, cinnamon, zest, and concentrate. Cover and microwave on HIGH for 3 minutes or until boiling.

Peel pears, but do not remove stem. Core just the bottom of the pear (the top of the pear remains closed to seal in the juices). Place pears in hot juice, cored side down in the juice. Cover and microwave on HIGH for 5 minutes. Turn pears over and place the stem end in the juice on HIGH for 2-1/2 minutes. You'll know pears are done when they retain their shape, but are fork-tender.

Total Calories Per Serving: 103 Total Fat as % of Daily Value: 0%
Protein: 1 gm Fat: <1 gm Carbohydrates: 26 gm Calcium: 15 mg
Iron: <1 mg Sodium: 2 mg Dietary Fiber: 5 gm

Tomatoes Au Gratin
(Serves 4)

Breakfast doesn't have to be sweet! Pair this dish with a bagel and some vegan sausage or bacon.

4 ripe but firm tomatoes (about 1-1/2 pounds)
2 teaspoons black pepper

4 Tablespoons dry breadcrumbs
4 Tablespoons shredded vegan cheese
2 teaspoons nutritional yeast (optional)

Cut tomatoes in half and place on a plate, cut side up. Sprinkle each tomato half with 1/2 teaspoon pepper, 1 Tablespoon breadcrumbs, 1 teaspoon parsley, 1 Tablespoon cheese, and 1/2 teaspoon yeast. Microwave on HIGH for 2 minutes or until tomatoes are tender and cheese is melted.

Total Calories Per Serving Without Yeast: 73   Total Fat as % of Daily Value: 2%
Protein: 2 gm   Fat: 2 gm   Carbohydrates: 14 gm   Calcium: 26 mg
Iron: 1 mg   Sodium: 125 mg   Dietary Fiber: 2 gm

Fresh Mint Tea
(Serves 3)

You'll think you're in the Casbah when you drink this tea.

4 cups water
1/2 cup fresh mint leaves, loosely packed (approximately 1 large bunch)
3 Tablespoons dry vegan sweetener
2 teaspoons loose green tea

Place water in a large container or 2-quart casserole and boil (this should take 3-4 minutes on HIGH, depending on your microwave). Place mint leaves, sweetener, and tea in the boiling water. Allow tea to steep for 3 minutes, stirring occasionally. Strain and pour into individual cups. If not still very hot, microwave on HIGH for 30 seconds.

Total Calories Per Serving: 56   Total Fat as % of Daily Value: 0%
Protein: 1 gm   Fat: <1 gm   Carbohydrates: 14 gm   Calcium: 50 mg
Iron: 2 mg   Sodium: 20 mg   Dietary Fiber: 1 gm

Moscow Tea
(Serves 3)

This tea will get you through a cold morning.

1 teaspoon orange juice concentrate
1/2 teaspoon dry vegan sweetener
2 Tablespoons instant tea (powdered)
1/4 teaspoon ground cloves
1/4 teaspoon cinnamon
4 cups water

In a small cup mix together all ingredients except the water. Stir well to combine. Set aside.

Place water in a large container or 2-quart casserole and boil. (This should take 3-4 minutes, depending on your microwave.) Stir tea mixture into water until well blended. Pour into individual cups. If not still very hot, microwave on HIGH for 30 seconds.

Total Calories Per Serving: 10   Total Fat as % of Daily Value: 0%
Protein: <1 gm   Fat: <1 gm   Carbohydrates: 2 gm   Calcium: 11 mg
Iron: <1 mg   Sodium: 12 mg   Dietary Fiber: <1 gm

Cinnamon Hot Chocolate
(Serves 4)

Enjoy this Southwestern-style hot beverage.

1 quart soy or rice milk
2 ounces unsweetened chocolate (about 4 Table-
    spoons)
1/4 cup vegan dry sweetener

1 teaspoon vanilla extract
2 teaspoons ground cinnamon

Place all the ingredients in a 2-quart container or bowl and
stir. Microwave on HIGH for 5 minutes or until hot. Stir
and serve.

Total Calories Per Serving: 207   Total Fat as % of Daily Value: 19%
Protein: 8 gm   Fat: 13 gm   Carbohydrates: 21 gm   Calcium: 41 mg
Iron: 3 mg   Sodium: 36 mg   Dietary Fiber: 6 gm

Good Ol' Fashioned Hot Cocoa
(Serves 3)

Make a double batch of this cocoa and take some to work or
school.

1/4 cup warm water
3 Tablespoons vegan dry sweetener
3 Tablespoons unsweetened cocoa powder
3 cups soy or rice milk

Place warm water, sweetener, and cocoa powder in a
1-quart bowl or container. Microwave on HIGH for
30 seconds. Remove and stir to combine ingredients.

Add milk to cocoa mixture and stir. Microwave on
HIGH for 5 minutes or until hot.

Total Calories Per Serving: 139   Total Fat as % of Daily Value: 8%
Protein: 8 gm   Fat: 5 gm   Carbohydrates: 19 gm   Calcium: 27 mg
Iron: 2 mg   Sodium: 36 mg   Dietary Fiber: 5 gm

Coffee or Decaf, on the Run
(Serves 1)

This beverage is very easy to prepare.

1 teaspoon instant coffee
6 ounces cold water

Put coffee in a cup and stir in water. Microwave on HIGH for 2 minutes or until very hot (don't let it boil). Remove from microwave, stir in milk and sweetener to taste, and sip slowly!

Total Calories Per Serving: 4   Total Fat as % of Daily Value: 0%
Protein: <1 gm   Fat: <1 gm   Carbohydrates: 1 gm   Calcium: 6 mg
Iron: <1 mg   Sodium: 6 mg   Dietary Fiber: 0 gm

Hot Energy
(Makes 2 four-ounce servings)

Here's another quick and easy beverage.

1 cup vanilla soy, rice, or almond milk
1 teaspoon nutritional yeast
1 teaspoon powdered soymilk (available at most
   natural and health food stores)
1 Tablespoon orange juice concentrate
1/2 cup vanilla or chocolate soy or rice ice cream

Place all ingredients in a large glass or in a blender and stir or process until well combined. Place in a microwave-safe cup or glass and microwave for 2 minutes or until hot.

Total Calories Per Serving: 163   Total Fat as % of Daily Value: 11%
Protein: 6 gm   Fat: 7 gm   Carbohydrates: 19 gm   Calcium: 15 mg
Iron: <1 mg   Sodium: 120 mg   Dietary Fiber: <1 gm

Hot Steamers
(Each variation of this recipe makes two 4-ounce servings)

You'll need a blender for these quick and easy recipes.

1 cup (8 ounces) vanilla soy, rice, or almond milk
Add a choice of:
a) 1/2 medium very ripe banana, sliced *or*
b) 1/2 cup fresh or frozen, thawed, sliced berries *or*
c) 1 teaspoon instant coffee and 2 teaspoons vegan dry sweetener *or*
d) 2 Tablespoons fruit preserves, such as strawberry or apricot *or*
e) 1 teaspoon vanilla extract plus 2 teaspoons vegan dry sweetener

Place milk and choice of added in flavor in a blender canister. Blend until well combined. Pour into a microwave-safe cup or glass and microwave on HIGH for 1 minute and 30 seconds or until thoroughly hot.

a) Total Calories Per Serving: 99   Total Fat as % of Daily Value: 3%
Protein: 4 gm   Fat: 2 gm   Carbohydrates: 19 gm   Calcium: 4 mg
Iron: <1 mg   Sodium: 1 mg   Dietary Fiber: 1 gm

b) Total Calories Per Serving: 63   Total Fat as % of Daily Value: 2%
Protein: 3 gm   Fat: 2 gm   Carbohydrates: 10 gm   Calcium: 12 mg
Iron: <1 mg   Sodium: 0 mg   Dietary Fiber: 2 gm

c) Total Calories Per Serving: 62   Total Fat as % of Daily Value: 2%
Protein: 3 gm   Fat: 1 gm   Carbohydrates: 9 gm   Calcium: 5 mg
Iron: <1 mg   Sodium: 2 mg   Dietary Fiber: 0 gm

d) Total Calories Per Serving: 93   Total Fat as % of Daily Value: 2%
Protein: 3 gm   Fat: 2 gm   Carbohydrates: 18 gm   Calcium: 4 mg
Iron: <1 mg   Sodium: 8 mg   Dietary Fiber: <1 gm

e) Total Calories Per Serving: 66   Total Fat as % of Daily Value: 2%
Protein: 3 gm   Fat: 1 gm   Carbohydrates: 9 gm   Calcium: 4 mg
Iron: <1 mg   Sodium: 2 mg   Dietary Fiber: 0 gm

APPENDIX ONE
The Perfectly Stocked Microwave Kitchen

Tools of the Trade

Just as you need to select the ingredients you know you will use, you need to select kitchen equipment with which you're comfortable. The recipes in this book require the minimum amount of equipment while still taking advantage of labor-saving devices. In Chapter One we discussed how to purchase a microwave. Here's a wish list of microwave accessories and gadgets, as well as food ingredients.

In Addition to the Microwave

A good knife (and a way to sharpen it) and cutting board, several mixing bowls, a small and a large frying pan, a large and a small pot (with lids), a colander or strainer, several baking dishes, a blender—along with the usual necessities such as can openers, stirring spoons, spatulas, storage containers, and a measuring cup and spoons— should do it. We're assuming you remember where the stovetop and the conventional oven are, and that they are in good shape (i.e., the stove burners stay lit and the oven actually heats up to the temperature at which you set it). Be sure to have a good supply of foil and plastic wrap or waxed paper on hand, as well as an assortment of storage containers for extra portions of foods and ingredients.

You may not need all of these items to succeed at microwave cooking, but the majority of them will come in handy. If you are really ambitious or living in tight cooking quarters and have decided to make microwave cooking your major mode of food preparation, than you can pare down the list. You'll need a measuring cup and spoons, a knife and cutting board, several bowls and plates, storage containers, and some of the microwave dishes listed below.

If you like kitchen gadgets, you can certainly find a use for a food processor, an electric mixer, an electric can opener, a spice grinder, a coffee (or tea) brewer, a dehydrator, and a barbecue grill. These are not necessary for the recipes in the book. A microwave is, of course, necessary for this book. We've included recipe directions for conventional and microwave cooking in Chapter Three.

A Little More Detail
Chefs are told that a good cook can prepare any dish with just a knife, cutting board, and some assorted pots, pans, and bowls. True, but there are some pieces of equipment that can improve efficiency and generally make life easier. Vegan foods require the same amount of chopping, slicing, and combining as any type of menu.

Depending on the size of your kitchen, you may already have many of these items. Again they are not required, just handy.

1. <u>Blender or food processor</u>: useful for puréeing soups and sauces, finishing salad dressings, and combining custards. You could use a manual food mill (or your mixer

219

may come with a mill or ricer attachment), but the blender or food processor allows you to choose from many different textures.

2. Mixer: mixing foods by hand can develop muscles (and frustration). Choose the mixer size best suited to your production size. Standard attachments are usually a paddle and a whisk. Other attachments may include a grinder (for vegetables such as potatoes) or a ricer.

3. Slicer: if you will be slicing a lot of veggies (eggplant, potatoes, tomatoes, onions, and zucchini), you may want to think about investing in a home slicer. This is really a luxury, but you may want to have one to save time.

4. Rice cooker: can also be used to steam other grains. Depending on the amount of rice you will be preparing every day, this device could come in handy. You can prepare rice in your microwave; however, if you are preparing several dishes at one time, you may want to free up the microwave for other items.

5. Knives and cutting boards: sharp sturdy knives are essential. Knives that fit your hand, are easy to sharpen, and easy to sanitize make kitchen work a little easier. You may want to have more than one cutting board.

Microwave Equipment Bells and Whistles

If your microwave does not have a built-in turntable, you may want to invest in a spring-driven turntable. Generally, you wind the spring-driven turntable and it slowly rotates for several minutes. This saves you from having to stop the microwave and turn the dishes.

There are many inserts and cooking attachments to assist in microwave cooking. For example, there is a bacon-cooker, which looks like a thick plastic plate with deep grooves. It is designed to allow the fat from bacon to drip away from bacon as it cooks. Vegans can use this insert to cook vegan bacon and veggie dogs and burgers. Any excess oil will drip away and give the burgers and veggie dogs a "grilled" look. There is an egg cooker insert, too, used to make micro-waved scrambled eggs and omelets. Vegan cooks can use this insert with tofu. You can microwave foods without these products, but they can make life easier if you prepare a certain type of microwaved food all the time.

Cookware

You will need at least a few dishes and plates for micro-wave cooking. Some of your everyday bowls and dishes may already be microwaveable. Below are examples of some of the cookware you may want to consider.

<u>Oven-safe glass or ceramic-like Pyrex™ or Corning Ware™ and lids</u>: you will have to check the sizes of the cookware against the size of your microwave's interior.

<u>Porcelain</u>: be careful of glazes. Many glazes contain metals, which could overheat or be flammable in a microwave. Do the dish test (listed below) to ascertain if your porcelain bowl or dish is microwave-safe.

<u>Dinnerware</u>: many of your favorite plates or bowls may be microwave-safe. Check the label or ask the manufacturer about this.

<u>Clay bakers or Tandoris</u>: if they'll fit into your microwave, you can use them. Soak clay bakers or Tandoris in cool water 15 minutes prior to use and drain it before putting it in the microwave. Clay bakers are good for foods that need to be heavily steamed, due to toughness or thickness. (Examples would be fresh beets or turnips, white or sweet potatoes, and most root vegetables.)

<u>Microwave-safe plastic cookware and lids</u>: this type of dish or bowl cooks faster than glass, but will warp or melt if it gets too hot. Be careful to inspect plastic cookware to be sure no burn marks have developed. If they have, do not use them for microwave cooking. Never use plastic margarine tubs, Styrofoam, or other non-microwave safe plastic for microwave cooking.

<u>Paper plates</u>: paper plates can be used on a one-time basis to reheat foods. Unfortunately, paper plates made from recycled paper can ignite, so avoid using them in the microwave.

<u>Glass or plastic measuring cups</u>: check the label or with the manufacturer to ascertain if these are microwave-safe. Measuring cups can be a convenient container to use in the microwave.

Thoughts on Stocking the Pantry

It's easier to prepare foods if you have adequate supplies on hand. Here are the vegan items we like to have in our refrigerator, freezer, and pantry:

1. Refrigerator: tofu (firm, silken), tempeh, seitan, soymilk, chocolate and vanilla rice milk, loads of fresh produce, fresh herbs (including ginger, garlic, basil, rosemary, and oregano), soy sauce or tamari, okara, tortillas, pita bread, assorted juices, hummus, salsa, and lemon juice

2. Freezer: extra firm tofu and tempeh, soy ice cream, frozen soybeans (edamame) and other veggies, apple and orange juice concentrate (in place of refined sugar), and extra vegetable stock

3. Pantry: canned tomatoes, salsa, mushrooms, soy beans, tomato purée, egg replacer, assorted flours, canned vegetable broth and favorite canned and dry soup mixes, several kinds of rice, dried herbs and spices, canned and dried beans and lentils, pasta, couscous, quinoa, kasha, baking powder, baking soda, cornstarch, vinegar, mustard, assorted oils, flavoring extracts, and zests.

Is this a lot of food? Definitely! You need to select the ingredients you will use the most and have them on hand. Frozen and dried ingredients generally have longer keeping times than fresh and refrigerated ingredients. You may want to plan your meals around your shopping schedule so you have lots of variety in ingredients without any waste or spoilage.

APPENDIX TWO
Vegan Glossary

The following definitions are included to assist you in shopping and preparing recipes. Some give you more information about various vegan products and others give details about less common cooking terms or products.

Almond Milk: This beverage is produced by expressing (pressing) almonds for their liquid. Look for almond milks that are fortified with vitamin A, vitamin D, and calcium. Can be used in most recipes that call for soy or rice milk.

Balsamic Vinegar: This vinegar has been aged in oak barrels. Balsamic can be aged anywhere from one month to several years. It is thought to have originated in Modena, Italy, and some of the best balsamic still is exported from there. Balsamic vinegar is almost syrupy in consistency, has a deep red color, and a complex flavor.

Dry Sweetener: Some vegans use refined white sugar and some choose not to, since white cane sugar may be processed with filtration equipment that contains animal products. There are many alternative products on the market, such as beet sugar, natural dried cane sugar (one of the brand names is Succanat™), dried maple sugar, and turbinado sugar. You need to try out the various types and see which works for you, in terms of taste and texture. For this book, wherever you see "dry vegan sweetener" listed as an ingredient, you may use sucrose (white sugar) or any vegan dry sweetening product. Don't substitute liquid sweeteners, because they will not yield the right texture in the recipes. Artificial sweeteners, such as Saccharin™, will not work in these recipes. Stevia, a natural derived sweetener, is too concentrated for cooking recipes (and at the time of this writing, was very expensive).

Edamame: "Edamame" is the Japanese name for fresh soybeans. Before they are dried, soybeans are green and can be steamed for a snack or for additions into soups, salads, casseroles, etc. Edamame may be available fresh at farmers markets or Asian markets and are available frozen in many grocery stores.

Liquid Sweeteners: Vegans avoid honey. Alternate types of sweeteners are dry sweeteners (explained above) and syrups such as rice syrup, malt syrup, and maple syrup. Puréed fruit, thawed orange juice and apple juice concentrate, apple sauce, and fruit butters (such as apple butter) can be used for sweetening.

Measurements: Just to refresh your memory
    3 teaspoons = 1 Tablespoon
    2 Tablespoons = 1 ounce
    1 cup = 8 ounces
    1/8 cup = 1 ounce or 2 Tablespoons
    1/4 cup = 2 ounces or 4 Tablespoons
    1/2 cup = 4 ounces
    3/4 cup = 6 ounces
    1 pint = 2 cups or 16 ounces
    1 quart = 4 cups or 32 ounces
    1 pound = 16 ounces

Nonreactive: When you are cooking, you don't want the material of the container to react with the ingredients.

This event may cause discoloring or the food will taste wrong. An example would be heating soymilk in an aluminum pan; the milk will turn gray. Nonreactive materials (where cooking is concerned) are plastic or glass.

Nut Butters: In addition to peanuts, nut butters are made from soybeans, almonds, cashews, hazelnuts, and pistachios, to name a few. Use as a sandwich spread, as a dessert topping, and as an ingredient in baking.

Nutritional Yeast: Nutritional yeast is a good source of vitamin B12 for vegans. Read the labels. Some nutritional yeasts are not vegan (may contain whey) and some don't contain B12. You can sprinkle nutritional yeast on hot or cold cereal, in soups, in baking batters and doughs, on cooked veggies, and in casseroles. Red Star Company makes a vegan "Vegetarian Support Formula™" nutritional yeast, which contains vitamin B12.

Pareve: This word indicates a kosher designation and is found on food labels. According to kosher tradition, pareve foods are "neutral." This information only helps a little when looking for vegan products, since pareve foods are allowed to contain eggs and fish.

Prepared Mustard: When you see this ingredient in a recipe, it means the mustard that comes ready to use (you know, the stuff you smear on your veggie hot dog at the ball park). This is opposed to dry mustard, which is a powder that you keep on your spice rack. Prepared mustard is a blend of ground mustard seeds, vinegar, turmeric (actual natural color, called "poor man's saffron"), and white pepper. Dry mustard is simply ground mustard seeds. It is important, when following a recipe, to use the form of mustard specified.

Rice Milk: This beverage is made by cooking and processing rice to manufacture a milky liquid. Look for rice milks that are fortified with calcium, vitamin A, and vitamin D. Rice milk can be used when soy, grain, or nut milks are called for in a recipe.

Seitan: Pronounced like the word *say* and *tan*, seitan is also called the "meat of the wheat." Made by extracting the gluten (or main protein) from wheat, seitan is chewy and stands up well to heat. Can be grilled as a "steak" or cut into pieces and stir-fried or baked. You can purchase seitan already made or make your own from seitan mixes.

Soy Cheeses: Read the label. Be sure that the "vegetarian or vegan cheese" (as they are often billed) does not contain lactose, milk solids, casein, whey, or rennet. If the package lists "enzymes," you may want to write to or call the manufacturing company to be sure that the enzymes are of plant or chemical origin.

Soy Crumbles: There are several frozen products that are sold as "soy crumbles." What we are suggesting are sausage-style, small pieces of soy (or tempeh or seitan) that can be used to add texture and flavor to recipes. If you can't find soy crumbles, make your own by crumbling soy sausage or vegan bacon strips or by slicing tofu dogs. We generally find soy crumbles in the frozen section with the breakfast items.

Soy Mayonnaise: You can purchase soy mayonnaise or make your own. Just be sure to keep it tightly covered while stored in the refrigerator. Discard homemade mayonnaise after 5 days. To make 1-1/2 cups of soy mayonnaise, drain 12 ounces of firm tofu. Place tofu in a blender and blend on high for 1 minute. Add 2 Tablespoons of lemon juice, 2 Tablespoons of rice syrup or liquid sweetener, 2 teaspoons of white vinegar, 1 teaspoon of prepared mustard, and 1 teaspoon of nutritional yeast (optional). Blend until smooth. Cover and refrigerate. It may need to be stirred before each use.

Soymilk: Soybeans are cooked and pressed for their liquid to create this milk. Soymilk is available in different percentages of fat and in various flavors. Look for soymilks that are fortified with calcium, vitamin A, and vitamin D. Enriched soymilk often contain vitamin B12 as well.

Soy Sour Cream: You can purchase soy sour cream or prepare your own. Simply purée 1 cup of silken tofu with 2 Tablespoons lemon juice until smooth. Cover and store in the refrigerator. Will last about 3 days.

Soy Substitutes: If you'd like to veganize some of your old recipes, the following chart should help:

Dairy or Meat Food Item	Soy Substitute
1 cup ricotta cheese	1 cup mashed firm tofu
1 cup milk	1 cup soy, rice, grain, or almond milk
1 large egg	2 Tablespoons puréed firm tofu
1 cup yogurt	1 cup soy yogurt or 1 cup puréed silken tofu with 1 Tablespoon lemon juice
1 cup sour cream	1 cup commercial soy sour cream or see recipe on previous page
1 ounce milk chocolate (for baking)	3 ounces (6 Tablespoons) unsweetened cocoa powder with 1 Tablespoon vegetable oil
1 pound ground beef (for sauces, etc.)	1 pound cubed firm tofu or 12 ounces (1-1/2 cups) crumbled seitan or tempeh
1 cup ice cream	1 cup sorbet or soy or rice "ice cream"

Tempeh: This item is fermented soy protein. It has a nutty, smoky taste, and a chewier, firmer texture than tofu. Use it on a grill, in the oven, or for stovetop sautéing. Available in various flavors.

Tofu: All tofu is made from pressed soybeans. Some tofu is processed with calcium, which can be from a vegan calcium source. You can purchase fresh tofu, which needs refrigeration, or aseptically packaged tofu, which does not need refrigeration until the package is opened. There are different textures and flavors of tofu. Tofu is already cooked, so you can simply take it out of the package and mix it with veggies and salsa or fruit and preserves. Remember that tofu is relatively neutral in flavor and will take on any flavor you give it. Firm tofu will hold its shape well. Cut it into cubes and toss it into salads, stir-fry or sauté it, or bake it. Silken or soft tofu can be blended for sauces, soups, smoothies, and salad dressings. Remember to refrigerate tofu as it is perishable.

Vegan Filled Pasta: Many pastas, such as ravioli, tortellini, and gnocchi, are filled. Read the labels to be sure the one you choose is vegan and stuffed with veggies such as potato, herbs, or soy products.

Vegan Tortillas: Some flour tortillas may be made with lard so read the labels and get to know the brands.

Vegetable Broth: This broth is a great substitute for chicken or meat broth. Make a batch and freeze it to use as needed.

(Makes about 1 quart or 4 servings)

1 teaspoon oil
1/2 cup chopped onion
1/4 cup chopped celery
1/4 cup chopped carrots
1/2 cup peeled, diced sweet potatoes
1/2 cup peeled, diced turnips or parsnips
2 cloves minced garlic

1 teaspoon dried thyme
1 bay leaf
1 quart water
1/2 teaspoon black pepper
1/4 cup minced fresh dill

Conventional Directions: Heat oil in a large pot and add onions, celery, carrots, potatoes, turnips, garlic, and thyme. Cook until browned. Add bay leaf and water and bring to a quick boil. Reduce heat, cover, and allow mixture to simmer until vegetables are very tender, about 35 minutes. Add pepper and dill, cook for 2 minutes. Remove from heat. If desired, broth can be strained and the vegetables used for soups or stews.

Microwave Directions: Place oil in a large bowl and add onions, celery, carrot, potatoes, turnips, garlic, and thyme. Toss until coated. Cover with waxed paper and microwave on HIGH for 6 minutes or until vegetables are soft. Add bayleaf and water, cover, and microwave on HIGH for 20 minutes or until flavors are combined. Add pepper and dill, and microwave on MEDIUM for 3 minutes. Remove from microwave, strain, and cool.

Note: This stock will last in the refrigerator for about 3 days or can be frozen for up to 2 months.

Total Calories Per Serving: 49   Total Fat as % of Daily Value: 2%
Protein: 1 gm   Fat: 1 gm   Carbohydrates: 9 gm   Calcium: 33 mg
Iron: 1 mg   Sodium: 31 mg   Dietary Fiber: 2 gm

Vegetarian Versus Vegan Products: Vegetarian products may contain eggs, cheese, dairy, or honey. Vegan products should not contain any animal products.

More Microwave Vegan Menus: Suggestions and Recipes for Holidays, Parties, and Entertaining

Holidays can be hectic times. When planning a holiday menu, be sure to include tried-and-true recipes along with new ones. Whatever you do, try a test run of any recipes you are going to include for an important event. Thanksgiving morning is not the time to try out a new microwave stuffing recipe.

Look through your everyday cookbooks and recipes and see what can be converted to the microwave method.

For example, mushroom gravy and garlic mashed potatoes can be made in the microwave, freeing up the stove and the oven for other foods. Try microwave-baked tomatoes filled with cornbread stuffing (add kernel corn, sautéed onions, carrots, celery, and toasted pine nuts to a traditional bread stuffing mix) or microwave braised kale (braised in vegetable stock and seasoned with onions and garlic).

Ready-to-use products, such as frozen vegan ravioli, can be microwaved and sauced and served as a hot or cold appetizer or entrée. Flavored tofu such as mesquite or teriyaki, or fake meats such as Tofurky™, can be sliced, covered with gravy, and microwaved for a convenient holiday entrée. Portobello mushrooms can be washed, coated with Italian dressing, and microwaved as holiday "steaks."

Here are some holiday menu ideas. Items that can be microwaved are denoted with an asterik (*).

Menu Ideas

Thanksgiving

Assorted cut vegetables and hummus
Herbed lentil loaf with mushroom gravy*
Mashed sweet potatoes with cranberry-walnut gravy*
Broccoli and cauliflower medley*
Tofu-pumpkin pie
Assorted cookies and fresh fruit
Or
Fresh winter squash soup*
Seasonal vegetable and onion pie with mushroom sauce*
Mashed sweet potatoes with praline topping*
Garlic mashed potatoes*
Glazed lemon carrots*
Apple-cinnamon cobbler*

233

Winter Holiday Meal
Tomato-lentil soup with fresh herbs*
Assorted ravioli with three-pepper sauce (peeled, puréed
    bell peppers used as a sauce)*
Baked penne with three mushrooms
Braised greens*
Mashed turnip and rutabagas*
Assorted breads and rolls
Lemon-tofu cheesecake

Happy New Year
Holiday hors d'oeurve platter (assorted olives, radishes,
    marinated veggies such as asparagus, cauliflower, arti-
    chokes, whole green onions, cherry tomatoes, cucumber
    and carrot sticks, assorted bread sticks, salsas, and dips)
Black-eyed peas and tofu (black-eyed peas are considered
    to bring good luck for the New Year)*
Mushroom risotto*
Red rose potatoes with olive oil and herbs*
Braised greens (braise greens of choice with white wine,
    minced garlic, and pepper)
Assorted sorbets and cookies

Fourth of July Grill-Out
Assorted veggie burgers (purchase commercially or make
    your own)
Veggie dogs*
Grilled lemon-herb tofu steaks
Corn on the cob* and baked white and sweet potatoes
    (cooked right in the coals)
Potato* and pasta salad (microwave potatoes for the salad)
Confetti broccoli slaw (can purchase shredded broccoli or
    you can do it)
Watermelon wedges and seasonal fresh fruit (served iced)

Halloween

Purée of carrot soup served in a pumpkin shell (scoop out pumpkin, toast seeds, and use toasted seeds as garnish)*

"Monster" sandwich consisting of a 6-foot submarine bread filled with grilled veggies, sliced tomatoes, onions, and peppers, etc.

Cole slaw and potato salad (if available, try purple potatoes)

Assorted veggie chips (bake thinly sliced potatoes, carrots, and beets) with flavored hummus

"Dirt and worms" dessert: frozen sorbet or other vegan frozen dessert mixed with cookie and cake crumbs, chopped raisins, and canned fruit cut into strips.

Easter

Fresh spinach salad with Mandarin orange segments, sliced almonds, and vinaigrette dressing

Stuffed tomatoes*

Brown rice pilaf with dates, raisins, and pineapple*

Baby carrots tossed with dill and margarine*

Broccoli and cauliflower florets tossed with garlic and lemon*

Peach upside down cake

Rosh Hashana

Mock chopped liver with assorted crackers

Mushroom barley soup*

Vegetarian kishke*

Stuffed baked potatoes

"Creamed" spinach (use puréed tofu and soymilk to create a "cream" sauce)*

Sliced carrots tossed with apple juice and parsley*

Sliced citrus (oranges, pink grapefruit, and tangerines, etc.)

Assorted fruit breads (carrot, zucchini, and pumpkin)

Curried Greens
(Serves 5)

Serve this combination as a colorful side dish for holiday entrées.

Vegetable oil spray
1/4 cup minced onions
1 clove garlic, minced
1/4 cup diced carrots
1/4 cup diced celery
1/2 cup vegetable stock
2 teaspoons curry powder
1 teaspoon white pepper
2 pounds frozen chopped greens, thawed (about
  5 cups)

Spray a microwave-safe 2-quart bowl with oil. Add onions, garlic, carrots, and celery and microwave for 2 minutes or until vegetables are soft. Add stock, curry powder, and white pepper and stir. Squeeze any remaining water from greens and add to bowl. Microwave uncovered for 5 minutes or until greens reach desired texture. Serve hot.

Note: Use frozen mustard, collard, turnip greens, or kale. If using fresh, wash, stem, and coarsely chop and adjust cooking time so that greens are cooked to desired texture.

Total Calories Per Serving: 51   Total Fat as % of Daily Value: 1%
Protein: 5 gm   Fat: 1 gm   Carbohydrates: 9 gm   Calcium: 223 mg
Iron: 3 mg   Sodium: 107 mg   Dietary Fiber: 7 gm

Micro-Steamed Belgian Endive
(Serves 3)

This mix is a delicate, elegant side dish that can be made with Belgian endive, or its crimson cousin, raddichio.

3 heads Belgian endive
2 Tablespoons fresh lemon juice
2 teaspoons vegan margarine, melted
1/2 cup vegetable broth

Place whole Belgian endive heads in a shallow microwave-safe pan. In a small cup, combine lemon juice, margarine, and broth. Pour evenly over endive. Cover and microwave on HIGH for 3 minutes. Uncover and turn the endive over. Re-cover and microwave on HIGH for 2 more minutes or until the endive is just tender. Serve whole or sliced.

Total Calories Per Serving: 55   Total Fat as % of Daily Value: 4%
Protein: 2 gm   Fat: 3 gm   Carbohydrates: 7 gm   Calcium: 140 mg
Iron: 1 mg   Sodium: 140 mg   Dietary Fiber: gm

Double Stuffed Green and Purple Potatoes

(Makes 8 side dishes or 10 appetizers)

This dish is colorful and flavorful.

2 pounds small purple potatoes (select the smallest
  ones: if purple potatoes aren't available, you can
  use red rose or white rose potatoes)
2 cups shredded fresh spinach leaves
3 Tablespoons vegan sour cream
2 Tablespoons vegan American or Cheddar cheese,
  shredded
2 teaspoons lemon juice
1 garlic clove, minced
2 teaspoons white pepper

Wash potatoes. Pierce each one with a fork and place on a
microwave-safe plate. Microwave on HIGH for 6-8 minutes
or until very tender. Set aside.

Place spinach in a large microwave safe bowl. Cover
with a dampened paper towel and microwave on HIGH for
3-4 minutes or until tender. Drain, if necessary.

Scoop out a small amount from the center of each potato. You can use a melon baller. Put the scooped-out pulp in a blender canister. Add spinach, sour cream, cheese, lemon juice, garlic, and pepper to the canister and process only briefly, just to loosely combine. You want a coarse mixture. Spoon the mixture into each potato. The potatoes can be served as is, which will be slightly warm. Or you can cover and chill them and serve cold. Or you can place them on a microwave-safe plate, cover them, and microwave on HIGH for 4-5 minutes or until hot.

Total Calories Per Serving: 104		Total Fat as % of Daily Value: 2%	
Protein: 2 gm	Fat: 1 gm	Carbohydrates: 23 gm	Calcium: 16 mg
Iron: <1 mg	Sodium: 102 mg	Dietary Fiber: 2 gm	

Individual Winter Squash with Mushroom and Spinach Stuffing

(Serves 4)

These beauties are almost too pretty to eat.

4 individual hard-shelled squash, such as Golden
  Nugget, or 2 large hard-shelled squash, such as
  Acorn
1/2 cup water
Vegetable oil spray
1-1/4 pounds mixed fresh mushrooms such as
  button, shiitake, and enoki, washed, dried and
  minced (about 4-1/2 cups)
1 garlic clove, minced
3/4 cup frozen chopped spinach, thawed, drained,
  and squeezed of most liquid
2 cups prepared tomato sauce
2 teaspoons dried basil
2 teaspoons dried oregano
1 teaspoon black pepper

Wash squash and pat dry. If you have individual squash, cut a slice off the top, lengthwise. If you have larger squash, cut in half.

Place squash halves, cut side down, on a microwave-safe dish. Add 1/2 cup water. Cover and microwave on HIGH for 10 minutes or until just tender. Remove and set aside.

240

Spray a 1-quart microwave-safe bowl with oil. Add remaining ingredients and mix well. Cover and microwave on HIGH for 4 minutes.

Drain the squash and scoop out the sides. Leave as much of the squash interior as possible. Fill each squash or squash half with the stuffing. Cover and microwave on HIGH for 5 minutes or until thoroughly heated.

Total Calories Per Serving: 178   Total Fat as % of Daily Value: 1%
Protein: 10 gm   Fat: 1 gm   Carbohydrates: 39 gm   Calcium: 133 mg
Iron: 5 mg   Sodium: 622 mg   Dietary Fiber: 9 gm

Cilantro-Marinated Tofu or Tofurky
(Serves 4)

Serve this savory entrée with green rice (cooked white or brown rice with chopped cilantro).

1/2 cup vinegar
2 Tablespoons olive oil
1 cup chopped fresh cilantro
1 Tablespoon red pepper flakes
2 garlic cloves, minced
1-1/2 pounds extra firm tofu, drained or 1-1/2
  pounds Tofurky™, cubed
Vegetable oil spray
1 cup chopped onions
1/2 cup minced red bell peppers
1/4 cup minced carrots
1/2 cup vegetable broth

Place vinegar, oil, cilantro, red pepper flakes, and garlic in a blender canister and process until puréed. If you like, save 1/4 cup of the marinade to pour over a rice accompaniment. Place marinade in a plastic or glass bowl and add tofu cubes. Cover and refrigerate for at least 2 hours. Spray a shallow microwave-safe pan with oil. Drain the tofu and discard the marinade. Place tofu in pan and top with onions, peppers, and carrots. Pour broth evenly over tofu. Cover and microwave on HIGH for 3 minutes. Turn cubes, re-cover, and microwave on HIGH for 4 more minutes or until vegetables are tender. Serve hot, over rice, couscous, or barley.

Savory Mushroom Gravy
(Makes about 1 pint)

This gravy is a "make ahead" dish, good for entrées, vegetables, grains, and potatoes. It can be made up to 2 days ahead of time and kept cold until ready to reheat.

1/4 cup dried mushrooms (about 5 Tablespoons)
1 Tablespoon minced onions
1/4 cup water
2 cups vegetable or mushroom stock or broth
2 Tablespoons finely chopped walnuts
1 teaspoon black pepper
1/2 teaspoon dried marjoram
1/4 teaspoon dried thyme
2 Tablespoons all-purpose flour or as needed

Combine dried mushrooms, onions, and water in a 1-quart microwave-safe bowl. Cover and allow to stand for 15 minutes. Keep covered and microwave for 2 minutes on HIGH. Stir and add remaining ingredients, except flour, and stir to combine. Cover and microwave on HIGH for 5 minutes. Allow to stand for 1 minute. Rapidly whisk in flour to thicken. If additional flour is needed for satisfactory thickness, add by teaspoonfuls. Cover and microwave on HIGH for 2 minutes or until heated.

The following three recipes require no cooking. They are excellent accompaniments for holiday meals.

Asian Spice, Asian Pear Salad with "Creamy" Apple Cider Dressing
(Serves 5)

This cool and shimmery dish goes well with spicy entrées.

Salad:
1 cup finely shredded Romaine
1 cup finely shredded red cabbage
2 cups cored and coarsely chopped Asian pears or Bartlett pears
1/4 cup black raisins
1/4 cup golden raisins

Dressing:
1/4 cup vegan mayonnaise or mayonnaise-based salad dressing
1/4 cup apple cider
1/2 teaspoon ground allspice or Chinese 5-spice powder

Combine romaine, cabbage, pears, and raisins in a large bowl and toss. In a small bowl, mix together mayonnaise, apple cider, and spice. Chill the salad and the dressing. Just before serving, drizzle the dressing on the salad and serve.

Note: Asian pears are also called Chinese apple-pears.

Total Calories Per Serving: 125   Total Fat as % of Daily Value: 9%
Protein: 1 gm   Fat: 6 gm   Carbohydrates: 20 gm   Calcium: 21 mg
Iron: 1 mg   Sodium: 46 mg   Dietary Fiber: 3 gm

Lemon-Parsley Apple and Cucumber Salad

(Serves 6)

Get sweetness, tang, and crunch from this elegant salad.

Salad:
6-8 lettuce leaves (for underliner)
2 cups cored and chopped green apples
2 cups peeled, deseeded, and chopped cucumbers
2 Tablespoons lemon juice
1 cup finely shredded fresh baby spinach leaves

Dressing:
1/2 cup olive oil
1/3 cup fresh lemon juice
2 Tablespoons chopped fresh parsley
1 teaspoon apple juice concentrate
1 teaspoon white pepper

Line individual salad plates or a salad platter with lettuce leaves. In a small bowl, toss together the apples, cucumbers, and lemon juice. Place on top of lettuce leaves. Sprinkle spinach leaves on top of apples. In a small bowl, whisk together all dressing ingredients until frothy. Pour evenly over salad and serve immediately.

Total Calories Per Serving: 196
Protein: 1 gm   Fat: 18 gm
Iron: 1 mg   Sodium: 10 mg

Total Fat as % of Daily Value: 28%
Carbohydrates: 9 gm   Calcium: 24 mg
Dietary Fiber: 1 gm

No Bake Pumpkin Tofu Custard

(Serves 5)

It's best to make this dessert a day ahead.

1 cup silken tofu, drained
1 cup canned pumpkin pie filling (unsweetened)
1/2 cup very ripe banana, sliced
2 Tablespoons orange juice concentrate
1 Tablespoon apple juice concentrate
1 teaspoon fresh orange zest
2 teaspoons ground cinnamon
1 teaspoon ground nutmeg
1 teaspoon ground ginger

Place all ingredients in a blender canister and process until smooth. Pour into 5 individual dessert cups. Refrigerate for at least 3 hours before serving.

Total Calories Per Serving: 121
Protein: 3 gm   Fat: 2 gm
Iron: 1 mg   Sodium: 116 mg

Total Fat as % of Daily Value: 3%
Carbohydrates: 25 gm   Calcium: 49 mg
Dietary Fiber: 6 gm

You'll find that many of these recipes can be used through-out the year. The kishka, spinach and mushroom kugel, and the sweet potato tzimmes are year-round favorites. Recipes were designed for a 800-1000 watt microwave with a turntable. If you have a lower-powered microwave, you may need to increase the cooking time. If you don't have a turntable, then rotate dishes half-way through cooking.

Pizza for Pesach
(Serves 1)

Makes a good entrée for lunch and even breakfast.

1 piece of matzo
3 Tablespoons tomato sauce
1 Tablespoon sliced green pepper
1 Tablespoon sliced fresh mushrooms
1 Tablespoon thinly sliced onions

Place matzo on a microwave plate or on a paper towel. Spread tomato sauce evenly on matzo. Pile on the vegetables. Microwave on MEDIUM (50%) for 2 minutes. Serve hot!

Total Calories Per Serving: 133   Total Fat as % of Daily Value: 1%
Protein: 4 gm   Fat: 1 gm   Carbohydrates: 29 gm   Calcium: 13 mg
Iron: 1 mg   Sodium: 279 mg   Dietary Fiber: 2 gm

Pesach Stuffed Derma (Kishka)

(Serves 6)

This kishka is not just for Passover, so you can make several batches of it and freeze them. This recipe is easier to make if you have a food processor or blender to do some of the chopping, but you can do it by hand.

1-1/2 cups minced onions
3/4 cup minced carrots
1/4 cup minced celery
1/2 cup oil
1 cup matzo cake flour
1 cup matzo meal
1/4 cup vegetable stock or water
1/2 teaspoon garlic powder
1 teaspoon paprika
1/2 teaspoon black pepper
1 teaspoon salt

If you have a food processor or blender, combine onions, carrots, celery, and oil in the canister and process until finely mixed. If you do not have a food processor, combine the ingredients in a large bowl and chop and mix until finely mixed. Add matzo flour and meal, stock, and spices and process or mix to a fine paste. Place mixture on a microwave-safe dinner plate (9-inch diameter) and shape into a small ring. Cover with waxed paper. Microwave on HIGH for 6 minutes or until the kishka is dry to the touch. Let stand for 5 minutes before slicing.

Total Calories Per Serving: 294   Total Fat as % of Daily Value: 28%
Protein: 4 gm   Fat: 18 gm   Carbohydrates: 30 gm   Calcium: 21 mg
Iron: 2 mg   Sodium: 419 mg   Dietary Fiber: 2 gm

Pizza Casserole for Pesach
(Serves 5)

This casaserole can be made a day ahead. Leftovers are good cold.

2 cloves garlic, minced
3/4 cup chopped onions
1/2 cup chopped green pepper
1/2 cup chopped red pepper
1/2 cup chopped fresh tomatoes
2 cups thinly sliced fresh mushrooms
1 Tablespoon oil
3-1/2 cups tomato sauce
5 pieces of matzo

In a medium-size microwave bowl, mix garlic, onions, red and green peppers, and mushrooms. Add oil and toss. Microwave on HIGH for 4 minutes or until veggies are tender. Spread 1 cup of sauce in the bottom of a medium-size (about 7x10-inch) glass casserole. Place half the veggies over the sauce. Place matzo over the veggies, trimming the matzo to fit snugly into the dish. Repeat this one more time. Place remaining sauce over top matzo. Cover with plastic wrap, piercing in two places to vent. For more consistent cooking, place casserole dish on a microwave-safe rack. Microwave on MEDIUM (50% power) for 10 minutes. Rotate casserole and microwave 5 more minutes. If sauce is not bubbly or veggies are not tender, then microwave uncovered on HIGH for 2 more minutes. Allow to stand for 10 minutes before cutting.

Total Calories Per Serving: 220   Total Fat as % of Daily Value: 6%
Protein: 7 gm   Fat: 4 gm   Carbohydrates: 43 gm   Calcium: 40 mg
Iron: 3 mg   Sodium: 1043 mg   Dietary Fiber: 5 gm

Spinach/Mushroom Kugel
(Serves 6)

Kugel can be served as an entrée, appetizer, or side dish.
It freezes well, so make a double batch. This recipe works
best with fresh spinach, but if you need to use frozen
spinach, purchase chopped spinach, allow it to thaw and
squeeze it dry. Skip over the first paragraph of instructions.

3 cups fresh spinach (about 12 ounces)
1 cup chopped onions
1/4 cup chopped celery
1/2 cup chopped green pepper
1/2 cup grated carrots
1 cup minced fresh mushrooms
1/2 cup oil
1 teaspoon black pepper
1 cup matzo meal

Wash spinach well, removing stems if necessary. Allow to
drain, but do not dry (extra moisture is necessary for the
microwaving). Put spinach in a 2-quart microwave-safe
casserole. Cover with lid or vented plastic wrap. Microwave
on HIGH for 3 minutes or until wilted. Let stand covered
for 3 minutes. Uncover and allow to cool. Squeeze dry and
chop coarsely. Set aside.

In the microwave casserole you would like to cook your
kugel in (a round or square medium casserole is fine), place
the onions, celery, peppers, and carrots. Microwave on
HIGH for 2 minutes. Stir, add in mushrooms and oil, and
combine well. Microwave on HIGH for 3 minutes. Add
black pepper and matzo meal. Combine well. Pack the
mixture into the casserole and cover. If available, place
casserole on a microwave-safe rack. Microwave covered on

HIGH for 10 minutes or until a knife inserted in the center comes out almost dry. Let stand for 10 minutes, then slice.

Total Calories Per Serving: 240   Total Fat as % of Daily Value: 28%
Protein: 4 gm   Fat: 18 gm   Carbohydrates: 17 gm   Calcium: 44 mg
Iron: 2 mg   Sodium: 32 mg   Dietary Fiber: 2 gm

A.M. Crunchies for Pesach
(Makes about 5 cups or 10 servings)

Use this recipe as a cold cereal for breakfast or as a fast snack. It stores up to 2 weeks in an airtight container.

1/4 cup oil
3/4 cup maple syrup
3 cups matzo farfel
1/2 cup coarsely chopped almonds
1/2 cup coarsely chopped pecans
1/2 cup raisins
1/4 cup chopped dates
1/2 teaspoon minced fresh ginger
1/4 teaspoon ground cinnamon

In a heat resistant, microwave-safe bowl, combine oil and syrup. Microwave on HIGH for 2 minutes, stirring once, until boiling. Add farfel and nuts and mix well, so dry ingredients are coated. Microwave on HIGH for 5 minutes, stirring twice. Mixture will be sticky when it comes out of the microwave. As it cools, it will become crisp.

Place in storage container and allow to cool, stirring several times to break up mixture. Stir in raisins, dates, ginger, and cinnamon. Store in airtight container.

Total Calories Per Serving: 257   Total Fat as % of Daily Value: 20%
Protein: 3 gm   Fat: 13 gm   Carbohydrates: 34 gm   Calcium: 41 mg
Iron: 1 mg   Sodium: 5 mg   Dietary Fiber: 2 gm

Sweet Potato and Raisin Tzimmes

(Serves 8)

This dish gets even better with age. Make it a day or two ahead and allow the flavors to marry.

2 pounds sweet potatoes, peeled (about 4-1/2 cups)
3 pounds carrots, trimmed and peeled (about 6 cups)
1/2 cup raisins
1/2 cup pitted prunes
1/2 cup chopped dates or dried figs
1/2 cup chopped dried apricots
2 Tablespoons orange juice concentrate
1/4 cup maple syrup
2 Tablespoons water

Slice sweet potatoes and carrots as thinly and evenly as you can. Place all ingredients in a 3-quart bowl or casserole and mix to combine. Cover and microwave for 20 minutes or until carrots and potatoes are tender, stirring once during cooking. Remove from microwave and let stand covered for 10 minutes before serving.

Note: Leftovers can be frozen for up to 3 months.

Total Calories Per Serving: 329   Total Fat as % of Daily Value: 1%
Protein: 5 gm   Fat: 1 gm   Carbohydrates: 83 gm   Calcium: 88 mg
Iron: 2 mg   Sodium: 104 mg   Dietary Fiber: 11 gm

Passover Toffee
(Makes about 1-1/2 pounds or 24 one-ounce servings)

This dish is great to serve with coffee to guests or to give as an edible holiday gift.

1/2 cup vegan margarine
1/2 cup maple syrup
1/2 cup vegan dry sweetener
3 cups matzo farfel or Passover cold cereal
1/2 cup sliced almonds
1/2 cup chopped pecans or other Passover nuts
Vegetable oil spray or oil

In a large bowl that is heat resistant, combine margarine, syrup, and sweetener. Microwave on HIGH for 5 minutes or until boiling. Stir once during cooking. Add farfel and nuts and stir well to combine. Microwave on HIGH for 4 minutes, stirring once. You will know the mixture is done if you can drop a spoonful of the mixture into cold water and it turns crisp. If it is not done, microwave for additional time.

Cover a baking sheet with foil. Spray or grease lightly. Spread the mixture in a thin, even layer on the sheet. Allow to cool for 5 minutes. Moisten your hands with cold water and press down on mixture to flatten it evenly. Allow to stand for at least one hour. Break into small pieces.

Total Calories Per Serving: 109   Total Fat as % of Daily Value: 10%
Protein: 1 gm   Fat: 7 gm   Carbohydrates: 12 gm   Calcium: 17 mg
Iron: <1 mg   Sodium: 47 mg   Dietary Fiber: 1 gm

APPENDIX FOUR
Microwave Maven

1. To shell walnuts, almonds, hazelnuts, or Brazil nuts: Mix 2 cups of unshelled nuts with 1 cup of cold water in a microwave-safe bowl. Cover with vented plastic wrap. Microwave on HIGH for 2 minutes or until water boils. Let stand for 1 minute to cool. Drain, dry with cloth or paper towels, and shell. If using chestnuts, cut an "x" through the shell before microwaving.

2. To melt jam or jelly: Remove lid from jar. Microwave 1/2 cup for 40 seconds on HIGH.

3. To get more juice from a lemon or lime: Microwave one lemon or lime for 15 seconds on HIGH. Roll on counter and squeeze.

4. To defrost 1 pound of frozen margarine: Microwave uncovered on DEFROST for 2 minutes.

5. Use wooden toothpicks or skewers for assessing doneness. Use wooden chopsticks for stirring.

6. Defrost frozen foods before using as an ingredient or cooking time will be thrown off.

7. A dinner plate of food will reheat in about 1-2 minutes on HIGH.

8. Vegetarian gelatin-like desserts can be made in the micro-wave. Mix 2 cups of water with a 3-ounce package of veggie gelatin mix in a 4-cup casserole. Microwave on HIGH for 5 minutes, stirring once. Veggie gelatin will become clear when it reaches a boil. Remove from micro-wave and refrigerate until set.

9. If you would like your casserole to be browned, prepare it in the microwave and then bake in a 400-degree oven for 10 minutes or until golden brown.

10. To reheat a 2-quart refrigerated casserole, microwave on HIGH for 10 minutes, stirring once or twice.

11. Here's your very own Play-Dough™: This recipe will keep in the refrigerator for up to 6 months. It has great texture, and although not tasty, is non-toxic and wonderful for creating all kinds of treasures.

2 cups water
Liquid food coloring
2-1/2 cups all-purpose flour
1-1/4 cups salt
4 teaspoons cream of tartar
1/2 cup vegetable oil

In a large bowl, combine water and food coloring. Set aside. In a large, microwave-safe bowl, combine flour, salt, and cream of tartar. Add oil. Gradually add water to make a soft, workable dough. (You may not need all the water.) Microwave on HIGH for 3 minutes, until thick. Knead dough while it is still warm. Store in an airtight container in the refrigerator.

12. To reheat a 2-quart frozen casserole, microwave for 20-30 minutes, stirring once or twice.

13. If you prepare your own baby food, you can freeze it in ice cube trays. Each cube holds about 2 Tablespoons. One cube will take 20-30 seconds on HIGH to thaw. Also stir well and test the temperature before feeding baby.

14. Ingredients that are allowed to come to room temperature will take less time to cook. Take ingredients out of the refrigerator about 5 minutes before cooking. Defrost frozen ingredients in the microwave right before using.

15. If foods tend to be overcooked on the edges, reduce heat to MEDIUM (50%) and double the cooking time.

16. When making half the amount of a recipe, reduce cooking time by 1/3; if doubling the recipe, increase time by 1/2 to 2/3.

17. Always check your food before the cooking time is over. Interrupt cooking and stir or taste to ensure that overcooking doesn't occur. Microwave cooking can differ depending on the moisture content of the food.

18. When possible, arrange food in a circle with thicker parts facing towards the outside of the dish.

Fast Microwave Guide

The following times are for a 800-1000 watt microwave with a turntable.

A. Defrosting **Setting** **Approximate Time**

<u>Breads and Bakery</u>

	Setting	Approximate Time
a. 1 bagel or muffin	HIGH	20 seconds
b. 1 pancake or waffle	HIGH	20 seconds
c. 1 unsliced loaf of bread	HIGH	1 minute
d. 1 whole baked pie	DEFROST	7-9 minutes

Note: To ensure a soft defrosted baked product, cover with a paper or cloth towel.

<u>Dinner and Side Dishes</u>

	Setting	Approximate Time
a. 1 veggie burger	DEFROST	1-2 minutes
b. 1 veggie dog	DEFROST	1-2 minutes
c. veggie meat (such as soy ground round, tempeh, seitan, etc.)	DEFROST	4 minutes/pound
d. 1 cup rice or pasta casserole	HIGH	2 minutes
e. 1 cup soup or pasta sauce	HIGH	10-12 minutes
f. 1-1/2 cup veggies	HIGH	6-8 minutes

B. Cooking	Setting	Approximate Time
Fresh Veggies and Fruit		
a. Asparagus spears	HIGH	5-6 minutes
b. Green or wax beans	HIGH	7-8 minutes
(Add 1/4 cup water per pound.)		
c. Broccoli spears	HIGH	6-7 minutes
d. Brussels sprouts	HIGH	6-7 minutes
e. Sliced carrots	HIGH	7 minutes
(Add 1/4 cup water per pound.)		
f. Cauliflower florets	HIGH	6-7 minutes
g. Whole button mushrooms	HIGH	4-5 minutes
h. Baked potato or sweet potato (For an 8-ounce potato, pierce skin in several places.)	HIGH	4-5 minutes
i. Sliced onions or bell peppers	HIGH	2-3 minutes
j. Spinach or other greens	HIGH	3-4 minutes
k. Tomatoes	HIGH	4-5 minutes
l. Zucchini	HIGH	5-6 minutes
m. Winter squash	HIGH	6-7 minutes
(hard-shelled squash, cut in quarters or small pieces, deseeded, cut side down)		
n. Apples or pears	HIGH	2 minutes
(for baked apples, cover with waxed paper)		
m. Apples	HIGH	7-9 minutes
(for applesauce, cover with waxed paper)		
n. Stewed dried fruit	HIGH	1 minute
(assorted dried fruit; add 1/2 cup water per pound.)		

Note: All times above are per pound. To retain steam, cover veggies with vented plastic wrap. Place all veggies and fruit (except for apples) on a shallow casserole or deep platter to retain natural juices. Fruit should be microwaved in bowls to retain all juices.

Cooking	Setting	Approximate Time
Other Foods		
a. Cooked cereals	HIGH	2 minutes
(for 1 serving, microwave in deep bowl or cup)		
b. Veggie burger or dog	HIGH	2 minutes
c. Lentil or grain loaf	HIGH	6-8 minutes
(for 1 pound, in a round shape)		
d. Rice	HIGH	5 minutes, then 12 minutes.

(For 1 cup uncooked rice, cook covered for 5 minutes, stir, then cook 12 minutes more.)

C. Reheating	Setting	Approximate Time
1. 1 bagel or muffin	HIGH	10-15 seconds
2. 1 slice fruit pie	HIGH	20 seconds
3. 1/2 cup sauce or syrup	HIGH	35 seconds
4. 1 veggie dog and bun	HIGH	30 seconds
5. 1 slice pizza	HIGH	45 seconds
6. 1 cup canned veggies	HIGH	2 minutes
7. 1 cup cooked rice or pasta	HIGH	1 minute
8. 1 cup soup	HIGH	2 minutes
9. 4 cups casserole (1 quart)	HIGH	4-6 minutes

Note: The chart above is for reheating foods that have been either defrosted or already cooked. This chart will not be sufficient for frozen or raw foods.

Using Leftovers
Leftovers are an inevitable part of meal planning. Someone gets home late from work or school, someone opts for popcorn instead of a regular meal, or you decide to take a gamble and double the recipe, and what have you got? Leftovers! The microwave is the perfect device to assist you with the use of leftovers.

Ideas for Using Leftovers

Leftover Item	Can Be Used For
Baked potatoes	Can be mashed with melted vegan margarine, heated soy-milk or vegetable stock and pepper for fast mashed potatoes (heat once you've mashed and mixed). Add seasonings such as crushed garlic or garlic powder, fresh or dried parsley, fresh or dried rosemary, chopped onions or onion powder, or curry powder for seasoned mashed potatoes. *or* Cut baked potatoes (peel on) into large chunks and toss lightly with olive oil, dried parsley, or dried basil. Microwave just to heat and you have a fast appetizer or side dish. Sprinkle on some nutritional yeast for extra flavor.

Leftover Item	Can Be Used For
Cooked beans	Combine with chopped canned tomatoes, prepared salsa, and leftover cooked vegetables. Heat in microwave until steaming hot and you have a hearty soup.
Cooked vegetables	Purée vegetables with a small amount of soft tofu. Taste and season with your favorite spices. Heat in microwave until bubbly.
Cooked pasta	Toss with leftover beans, tomatoes or vegetables, and add some herbs and spices and a little bit of tomato sauce for a fast entrée.
Chili beans	Mix with leftover rice, chopped tomatoes, and chopped onions and/or peppers. Heat until hot for a new chili casserole. Thin this with vegetable juice and you have chili soup.
Baked sweet potatoes	Mash with a small amount of vegan margarine, add raisins, chopped pineapple, cinnamon, nutmeg, or ginger, and microwave until hot. These mashed sweet potatoes are served as a side dish or used as a pie filling.

Leftover Item	Can Be Used For
Canned peaches or pears	In a microwave-safe bowl, toss canned fruit (not drained) with oats, chopped nuts, dried fruit, and cookie or cake crumbs (optional). Microwave until bubbly and serve as a fast fruit cobbler.

Look at "underutilized portions of food" as a culinary challenge, not at household burden. You may find your leftover dishes are even better than the original dishes!

THE VEGETARIAN RESOURCE GROUP CATALOG

The following resources can be purchased from The Vegetarian Resource Group, PO Box 1463, Baltimore, MD 21203. You can order online at <www.vrg.org>, or charge your order over the phone by calling (410) 366-8343 between 9 am and 5 pm EST Monday through Friday.

Shipping and Handling Charges:

Orders under $25	$5 ($9 for Canada/Mexico)
Orders over $25	Free in continental U.S.
Foreign orders	Inquire first

SIMPLY VEGAN
QUICK VEGETARIAN MEALS

The immensely popular *Simply Vegan*, by Debra Wasserman and Reed Mangels, PhD, RD, is much more than a cookbook. It is a guide to a non-violent, environmentally sound, humane lifestyle. It features over 160 vegan recipes that can be prepared quickly, as well as an extensive nutrition section. The chapters cover topics on protein, fat, calcium, iron, vitamin B12, pregnancy and the vegan diet, and raising vegan kids. Additionally, the book includes sample menus and meal plans. There is also information on cruelty-free shopping by mail, including where to buy vegan food, clothing, cosmetics, household products, and books.

Available for $13. (224 pages)

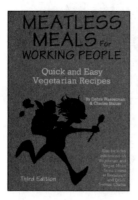

MEATLESS MEALS FOR WORKING PEOPLE
QUICK AND EASY VEGETARIAN RECIPES

Meatless Meals For Working People, by Debra Wasserman and Charles Stahler contains over 100 delicious fast and easy recipes, plus ideas which teach you to be a vegetarian within your hectic schedule using common convenient vegetarian foods. This handy guide also contains a spice chart, party ideas, information on quick service restaurant chains, and much more.

Available for $12. (192 pages)

VEGAN MEALS FOR ONE OR TWO
YOUR OWN PERSONAL RECIPES

Each recipe in *Vegan Meals for One or Two*, by Nancy Berkoff, EdD, RD, is designed so that you can realistically use ingredients the way they come packaged from the store when cooking for one or two. Meal planning and shopping information is included, as well as breakfast ideas, one-pot wonders, recipes that can be frozen for later use, grab-and-go suggestions, everyday and special occasion entrées, plus desserts and snacks. A glossary is provided.

Available for $15. (216 pages)

ORDER USING THE FORM ON PAGE 271

NO CHOLESTEROL PASSOVER RECIPES

Featuring 100 Vegetarian Passover Dishes, the *No Cholesterol Passover Recipes,* by Debra Wasserman is a must for every home that wants to celebrate a healthy and ethical Passover. Enjoy egg-less blintzes, dairy-free carrot cream soup, festive macaroons, apple latkes, sweet and sour cabbage, knishes, vegetarian chopped "liver," no-oil lemon dressing, eggless matzo meal pan-cakes, and much more.

Available for $9. (96 pages)

VEGAN PASSOVER RECIPES
EGGLESS & DAIRY-FREE DISHES

Vegan Passover Recipes, by Nancy Berkoff, EdD, RD, offers a plethora of eggless and dairy-free options for a healthy and great-tasting Festival of Freedom, including soups, salads, side dishes, sauces, entrées, and desserts. All recipes are suitable for Ashkenazi Eastern European Jewish tradition, which does not use beans or rice.

Available for $6. (48 pages)

OR ONLINE AT <WWW.VRG.ORG/CATALOG>

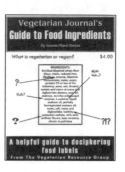

VEGAN IN VOLUME
VEGAN QUANTITY RECIPES FOR EVERY OCCASION

Vegan in Volume, by Nancy Berkoff, EdD, RD, is a 272-page book. It has 125 quantity recipes for every occasion. Chef Nancy Berkoff offers help with catered events, weddings, birthdays, college food service, hospital meals, restaurants, dinner parties, etc. She shares her knowledge of vegan nutrition, vegan ingredients, menus for seniors, breakfast buffets, desserts, cooking for kids, and much more.

Available for $20. (272 pages)

VEGETARIAN JOURNAL'S FOODSERVICE UPDATE

The Vegetarian Resource Group publishes *Vegetarian Journal's Foodservice Update*, a quarterly newsletter devoted to food service. It is edited by Chef Nancy Berkoff, EdD, RD and Debra Wasserman.

Subscriptions in the USA are $20 per year or $30 for one year of *Foodservice Update* and *Vegetarian Journal*.

OR ONLINE AT <WWW.VRG.ORG/CATALOG>

SUBSCRIBE TO VEGETARIAN JOURNAL

The practical magazine for those interested in health, ecology, and ethics.

<u>Inside each issue find</u>:

Nutrition Hotline — answers to your questions about vegetarian diets.

Lowfat Vegan Recipes — quick and easy dishes, international cuisine, and gourmet meals.

Natural Food Product Reviews

Scientific Updates — recent scientific papers relating to vegetarianism.

Vegetarian Action — individuals and groups incorporating vegetarianism into their lives and communities.

VEGETARIAN JOURNAL (ISSN 0885-7636) is published quarterly by the independent Vegetarian Resource Group.

Yes! I want to receive *Vegetarian Journal!*

Name: _____

Address: _____

City: _____ State: _____ Zip:_____

☐ Payment Enclosed (check or money order)

☐ Please charge my (circle one) MasterCard / Visa:

_____ Expires: ____ / ____

In the **U.S.**, send **$20** for one year of the quarterly *Vegetarian Journal*; in **Canada and Mexico,** please send **$32;** other **foreign subscribers,** please send **$42** in U.S. funds or via MasterCard or Visa. Send payment and subscription information to The Vegetarian Resource Group, PO Box 1463, Baltimore, MD 21203. Or fax this form to (410) 366-8804. You can order online at **<www.vrg.org/journal/subscribe.htm>**. Please e-mail **vrg@vrg.org** with any questions.

ORDER MORE COPIES OF VEGAN MICROWAVE COOKBOOK FOR $16.95 EACH!

Use or photocopy the form below to order *Vegan Microwave Cookbook* or any other materials published by The Vegetarian Resource Group.

Vegetarian Resource Group *Order Form*

Name: _____

Address: _____

City: _____ State: _____ Zip: _____

Phone: _____ E-mail: _____

Item:	Quantity:	Price:	Subtotal:
_____	_____	$_____	$_____
_____	_____	$_____	$_____
_____	_____	$_____	$_____
_____	_____	$_____	$_____

SHIPPING INFORMATION

For orders under $25, add $5 in the U.S. and $9 in Canada and Mexico. Shipping is free for orders over $25 in the continental U.S. For all other foreign orders, please inquire first.

Subtotal: $_____

Shipping: $_____

MD Residents Add 5% Sales Tax: $_____

Donation: $_____

Total: $_____

☐ Payment Enclosed (check or money order)

☐ Please charge my (circle one) MasterCard / Visa:

\# _____ Expires: ____ / ____

Send order information and payment to The Vegetarian Resource Group, PO Box 1463, Baltimore, MD 21203. Or fax this form to (410) 366-8804. You can order via telephone at **(410) 366-8343** Monday through Friday from 9 am to 5 pm EST or online at **<www.vrg.org>**. Please e-mail **vrg@vrg.org** with any questions.

INDEX BY SUBJECT

Almond Milk, 224
A.M. Microwave Tips, 197
Appetizers and Side Dishes, 136-173
Baking in the Microwave, 50
Balsamic Vinegar, 224
Bars and Fudge, 66 and 104-105
Biscuits and More, 99-105
Breakfast, 197-212
Buying the Microwave, 19
Casseroles, 56-61
Cleaning the Microwave, 24
Converting Traditional Recipes to the Microwave, 45-67
Cooking in a Microwave, 258-259
Cooking Pasta, 110
Cookware, 221
Daily Vegan Meal Planning, Basic Information for, 36-37
Defrosting in a Microwave, 257
Desserts, 62, 66, 76-83, 86-97, 104-105
Dips, 191-196
Dish Test, 15
Dressings, 191-196
Dry Sweetener, 224
Easter, 235
Edamame, 225
Entrées, 106-135
Estimating Time and Testing for Doneness, 48
Fast Microwave Guide, 257
Fourth of July Grill-Out, 234
Guide for Baking Muffins on HIGH Power, 84
Halloween, 235
Holidays, Parties, and Entertaining, 232-253
Hot Beverages, 213-217
Hot Sandwiches, 55
How to Build a Meal Around an Entrée, 106
How Microwaves Work, 11
Ideas for Using Leftovers, 260-262
Ingredient Tips, 48
Ingredients that Don't Work, 51
Kitchen Safety, 30
Liquid Sweeteners, 225
Loaves and "Meat" Balls, 107
Measurements, 225
"Meat" Ball Cooking Tips, 108
"Meat" Ball Recipe Variations, 109
Microwave Baking and Desserts, 68-105
Microwave Baking Techniques, 70
Microwave Cooking Terms, 12
Microwave Cooking Times, 14
Microwave Creativity, 40
Microwave Don'ts, 17

Microwave Equipment Bells and Whistles, 220
Microwave Maven, 254-262
Microwave Meal Planning, 39
Microwave Safety, 21
Microwave Settings, 15
Microwave-Soaking Dried Beans and Legumes, 176
More Ideas for Vegan Microwave Meals, 42
Muffins and Pies, 84-93
New Year Menu, 234
Nonreactive, 225
Nut Butters, 226
Nutritional Yeast, 226
Pareve, 226
Passover Microwave Recipes, 247-253
Perfectly Stocked Microwave Kitchen, The, 218-223
Pie Fillings, 92-93
Pots and Pans, 22
Preface, 9
Prepared Mustard, 226
Preparing Hot Desserts, 69
Puddings and Hot Fruit, 94-98
Quick Breads, 76-83
Reheating in a Microwave, 259
Rice Milk, 227
Rosh Hashana, 235
Sample Menu, 38
Sauces and Toppings, 72-75
Seitan, 227
Selecting Microwave Cooking from Conventional Methods, 47
Soups, 52-54, 174-190
Soy Cheeses, 227
Soy Crumbles, 227
Soy Mayonnaise, 228
Soymilk, 228
Soy Sour Cream, 228
Soy Substitutes, 229
Stocking the Pantry and Refrigerator, 25
Storing Leftovers, 23
Tempeh, 229
Thanksgiving, 233
Thoughts on Stocking the Pantry, 223
Tofu, 230
Tools of the Trade, 218
Using Leftovers, 260-262
Vegan Filled Pasta, 230
Vegan Glossary, 224-231
Vegan Menu Planning, 32-44
Vegan Tortillas, 230
Vegetable Broth, 230
Vegetarian Versus Vegan Products, 231
Winter Holiday Meal, 234

INDEX BY RECIPE

Appetizers and Side Dishes (Also see Holidays, Parties, and Entertaining)
Baked Corn, Baked Bean Style, 157
Baked Potatoes, 144
Beet Greens and Green Onions, 165
"Boiled" Potatoes, 145
Brussels Sprouts Mediterranean, 170
Cabbage and Caraway, 169
Coriander Kale with Slivered Carrots, 164
Cranberry Winter Squash, 159
Creamy Garlic Rice with Parsley and Onions, 153
Creamy Spinach, 155
Double Orange Carrots, 156
Easy Zucchini, 172
Garlic Spinach with Sesame, 161
Golden Carrots, 160
Green Steamed Kohlrabi, 163
Hot Potato and Caraway Salad (Vegan German Potato Salad), 150
Individual Microwave Pizzas, 142
Mashed Potatoes, 146
Mashed Potatoes with Rutabagas, 147
Okra Bayou, 166
Oktoberfest Sweet and Sour Red Cabbage with Green Apples, 168
Orange Rice with Celery, 151
Orange Snow Peas with Cashews, 167
Parsley and Soy Cauliflower, 158
Peas with Mushrooms and Onions, 171
Pizza Potatoes, 149
Snow Peas with Pine Nuts, 168
Soy Sauce Broccoli with Garlic and Hazelnuts, 162
Spicy Toasted Nachos, 139
Spinach Rice with Almonds, 154
Stuffed Baked Potatoes, 148
Stuffed Mushrooms or Cherry Tomatoes, 140
Sweet Potatoes in Orange Shells, 152
Vegan Chopped Liver, 143
Whole Spaghetti Squash, 173

Baked Goods (Also see Biscuits, Quick Breads, and Muffins and Pies)
Corn Bread, 64
Crispy Date Bars, 104
Peanut Butter Oatmeal Cookie Bars, 62

Beverages
Cinnamon Hot Chocolate, 214
Coffee or Decaf, On the Run, 216
Fresh Mint Tea, 213
Good Ol' Fashioned Hot Cocoa, 215
Hot Cocoa, 67
Hot Energy, 216

Hot Steamers, 217
Moscow Tea, 214

Biscuits
Baking Powder Biscuits, 103
Cinnamon Coffee Cake Biscuits, 102
In the Pantry Biscuits, 99
Marmalade Morning Biscuit Cake, 101
Ready-to-Bake Biscuits, 100

Breakfast
A.M. Poached Pears, 212
Baked Raisins and Apricots, 211
Blueberry Sauce, 204
Citrus Dried Plums, 208
Cornmeal Mini-Soufflés, 201
Dried Fruit Stew, 206
French Toast Matzo, 203
Gingery Figs, 210
Hominy Grits, 200
Hot Applesauce, 205
Hot Cornmeal Cereal, 200
Hot Fruit Stew, 210
Matzo Meal Mini-Soufflés, 202
Micro-Broiled Grapefruit, 208
Oatmeal for One, 199
Oatmeal for the Whole Crew, 199
Rhubarb Sauce, 206
Rice for Breakfast, 204
Spicy Dried Fruit Compote, 209
Stewed Fresh Rhubarb, 207
Tomatoes Au Gratin, 212

Casseroles
Casserole with Uncooked Potatoes, 58
Mixed Beans and Macaroni Casserole, 56
Tomato-Baked Beans, 60
Tri-Colored Stuffed Summer Squash, 59

Desserts (See Baked Goods, Fudge, Muffins and Pies, Pie Fillings, Puddings and Hot Fruit, and Quick Breads)

Dips and Salad Dressings
Avocado Dip (Guacamole), 191
Baba Ganoujh (Garlic-Eggplant Dip), 192
Capanata, 194
Spinach and Parsley Salad Dressing, 195
Tri-Color Herbed Peppers, 196
Tzatziki (Greek Cucumber Dip), 193

Entrées (Also see Holidays, Parties, and Entertaining and Sandwiches)
Baked Eggplant, 120
Barley and Mushroom Casserole, 128
Bulgur Pilaf, 129
Fast "Fried" Rice, 125
Microwave Lasagna, 116
Mushroom and Hazelnut Snacking Balls, 133
Mushroom Pasta, 122
Rice Casserole, 127
Scrambled Mushroooms with Tofu and Curry, 115
Southwestern-Influenced Rice and Pepper Medley, 112
Spanish-Style Rice, 126
Spinach Lasagna, 118
Stuffed Tomatoes Mediterranean, 114
Summer Squash and Eggplant Stew (Ratatouille), 119
Taco Salad, 113
Teenie Beenie Weenies, Updated, 124
Tofu Balls with Sauerkraut and Mustard, 132
Vegan Kishka, 121
Vegan Sausage and Creamy Potatoes, 123
Veggie Balls, 134
White Cupboard Chili, 111

Fudge
Chocolate Fudge, 66
Graham Cracker Toffee Fudge, 105

Holidays, Parties, and Entertaining (Also see Passover Dishes)
Asian Spice, Asian Pear Salad with "Creamy" Apple Cider Dressing, 244
Cilantro-Marinated Tofu or Tofurky, 242
Curried Greens, 236
Double Stuffed Green and Purple Potatoes, 238
Individual Winter Squash with Mushroom and Spinach Stuffing, 240
Lemon-Parsley Apple and Cucumber Salad, 245
Micro-Steamed Belgian Endive, 237
No-Bake Pumpkin Tofu Custard, 246
Savory Mushroom Gravy, 243

Muffins and Pies (Also see Pie Fillings)
Corn and Chili Muffins, 89
Ginger Snap Crust, 91
Make-Ahead Muffins, 88
Maple and Molasses Bran Muffins, 86
Peanut Butter Muffins, 90

Passover Dishes
A.M. Crunchies for Pesach, 251
Passover Toffee, 253
Pesach Stuffed Derma (Kishka), 248
Pizza Casserole for Pesach, 249
Pizza for Pesach, 247
Spinach/Mushroom Kugel, 250
Sweet Potato and Raisin Tzimmes, 252

Pie Fillings
Apple Pie, 92
Raisin Pie, 93

Puddings and Hot Fruit
Apple Betty, 97
Chocolate-Covered Bananas, 98
Mocha Bread Pudding, 96
Quick-Baked Apple, 95
Scandinavian Dried Fruit Dessert, 94

Quick Breads
Banana Bread, 80
Creamy Ginger and Date Bread, 83
Fruit and Nut Bread, 77
Gingerbread, 76
Graham Cracker Molasses Bread, 82
Pumpkin Bread, 78
Raisin and Orange Cake, 81

Salad Dressings (See Dips and Salad Dressings)

Sandwiches
Chili Cheese Dogs, 55
Reuben-Style Sandwich, 130
Toasted Peanut and Apple Sandwich, 131

Sauces and Toppings
Blueberry Sauce, 205
Crunchy Granola, 74
Orange Sauce, 74
Peanut Butter-Fudge Sauce, 73
Rhubarb Sauce, 206
Strawberry Sauce, 72

Side Dishes (See Appetizers)

Soups
Broccoli and Cheese Soup, 180
Cream of Cauliflower, 178
Creamy Pumpkin Soup, 184
Cucumber and Avocado Soup, 190
Fast Barley Soup, 183
Fresh Summer Squash Soup, 182
Potato and Asparagus Vichyssoise (Cold Potato and Asparagus Soup), 188
Potato Crecy, 179
Red Pepper Soup, 185
Russian Beet Borscht, 186
Split Pea Soup, 53
Vegetable-Corn Soup, 54
Vegetable Stock, 177

INDEX BY MAJOR INGREDIENT

Apple Juice
Dried Fruit Stew, 206

Apples
Apple Betty, 97
Apple Pie, 92
Hot Applesauce, 205
Lemon-Parsley Apple and Cucumber Salad, 245
Oktoberfest Sweet and Sour Red Cabbage with Green Apples, 168

Apricots (Dried)
Baked Raisins and Apricots, 211

Asparagus
Potato and Asparagus Vichyssoise (Cold Potato and Asparagus Soup), 188

Avocados
Avocado Dip (Guacamole), 191
Cucumber and Avocado Soup, 190

Baked Beans, Vegetarian
Teenie Beenie Weenies, Updated, 124

Bananas
Banana Bread, 80
Chocolate-Covered Bananas, 98
Hot Sundaes, 70

Barley
Barley and Mushroom Cassserole, 128
Fast Barley Soup, 183

Beans (Also see Kidney, Pinto or Red Beans, and White Beans)
Mixed Beans and Macaroni Casserole, 56

Belgian Endive
Micro-Steamed Belgian Endive, 237

Bell Peppers
Red Pepper Soup, 185
Tri-Color Herbed Peppers, 196

Beet Greens
Beet Greens and Green Onions, 165

Beets
Russian Beet Borscht, 186

Blueberries (Fresh or Frozen)
Blueberry Sauce, 204

Bran Flakes
Make-Ahead Muffins, 88
Maple Molasses Bran Muffins, 86

Bread
Apple Betty, 97
Individual Microwave Pizzas, 142
Mocha Bread Pudding, 96
Reuben-Style Sandwich, 130
Stuffed Tomatoes Mediterranean, 114
Toasted Peanut and Apple Sandwich, 131

Bread Crumbs
Tofu Balls with Sauerkraut and Mustard, 132
Veggie Balls, 134

Broccoli (Fresh or Frozen)
Broccoli and Cheese Soup, 180
Soy Sauce Broccoli with Garlic and Hazelnuts, 162

Brussels Sprouts (Frozen)
Brussels Sprouts Mediterranean, 170

Bulgur
Bulgur Pilaf, 129

Cabbage
Cabbage and Caraway, 169
Oktoberfest Sweet and Sour Red Cabbage with Green Apples, 168

Carrots
Asian Spice, Asian Pear Salad with "Creamy" Apple Cider Dressing, 244
Double Orange Carrots, 156
Golden Carrots, 160
Pesach Stuffed Derma (Kishka), 248
Potato and Asparagus Vichyssoise (Cold Potato and Asparagus Soup), 188
Potage Crecy, 179
Sweet Potato and Raisin Tzimmes, 252
Vegan Kishka, 121
Vegetable-Corn Soup, 54

Carrots (Canned)
Veggie Balls, 134

Cauliflower
Cream of Cauliflower, 178
Parsley and Soy Cauliflower, 158

Celery
Mixed Beans and Macaroni Casserole, 56
Orange Rice with Celery, 151
Vegetable Stock, 177

Cheese, Vegan
Baked Eggplant, 120
Broccoli and Cheese Soup, 180
Individual Microwave Pizzas, 142
Microwave Lasagna, 116
Reuben-Style Sandwich, 130
Spicy Toasted Nachos, 139
Spinach Lasagna, 118
White Cupboard Chili, 111

Chocolate or Carob, Vegan (Bars, Chips, Powder)
Chocolate-Covered Cherry Fudge, 70
Chocolate-Covered Granola Sundaes, 70
Chocolate Fudge, 66
Hot Cocoa, 67
Peanut Butter-Fudge Sauce, 73
Peanut Butter Oatmeal Cookie Bars, 62

Cilantro
Cilantro-Marinated Tofu or Tofurky, 242

Corn
Baked Corn, Baked Bean Style, 157
Vegetable-Corn Soup, 54

Cornmeal
Corn Bread, 64
Cornmeal Mini-soufflés, 201
Hot Cornmeal Cereal, 200

Cranberry Juice
A.M. Poached Pears, 212

Cucumbers
Cucumber and Avocado Soup, 190
Lemon-Parsley Apple and Cucumber Salad, 245
Tzatziki (Greek Cucumber Dip), 193

Dates
Crispy Date Bars, 104
Fruit and Nut Bread, 77

Deli Slices, Vegan
Reuben-Style Sandwich, 130

Eggplant
Baba Ganoujh (Garlic-Eggplant Dip), 192
Baked Eggplant, 120
Capanata, 194
Summer Squash and Eggplant Stew (Ratatouille), 119

Figs
Gingery Figs, 210

Graham Crackers, Vegan
Graham Cracker Toffee Fudge, 105

Granola, Vegan
Chocolate-Covered Granola Sundaes, 70

Grapefruit
Micro-Broiled Grapefruit, 208

Green Beans (Canned or Frozen)
Vegan Chopped Liver, 143
Veggie Balls, 134

Greens (Also see Beet Greens or Kale)
Curried Greens, 236

Grits
Hominy Grits, 200

Hot Dogs, Vegan
Chili Cheese Dogs, 55
Teenie Beenie Weenies, Updated, 124
Vegan Sausage and Creamy Potatoes, 123

Kale
Coriander Kale with Slivered Carrots, 164

Kidney Beans
Taco Salad, 113
Teenie Beenie Weenies, Updated, 124

Kohlrabi
Green Steamed Kohlrabi, 163

Mandarin Oranges
Double Orange Carrots, 156

Maple Syrup
Maple Molasses Bran Muffins, 86

Matzo
French Toast Matzo, 203
Pizza Casserole for Pesach, 249
Pizza for Pesach, 247

Matzo Farfel
A.M. Crunchies for Pesach, 251
Passover Toffee, 253

Matzo Meal
Matzo Meal Mini-Soufflés, 202
Pesach Stuffed Derma (Kishka), 248
Spinach/Mushroom Kugel, 250
Vegan Kishka, 121

Milk, Vegan (Soy, Rice, Nut, or Grain)
Chocolate Fudge, 66
Cinnamon Hot Chocolate, 214
Corn Bread, 64
Cornmeal Mini-Soufflés, 201
Cream of Cauliflower, 178
Creamy Garlic Rice with Parsley and Onions, 153
Creamy Pumpkin Soup, 184
Good Ol' Fashioned Hot Cocoa, 215
Hot Cocoa, 67
Hot Energy, 216
Hot Steamers, 217
Make-Ahead Muffins, 88
Maple Molasses Bran Muffins, 86
Matzo Meal Mini-Soufflés, 202
Mocha Bread Pudding, 96
Potato and Asparagus Vichyssoise (Cold Potato and Asparagus Soup), 188
Spinach Rice with Almonds, 154

Mint (Fresh)
Fresh Mint Tea, 213

Molasses
Maple Molasses Bran Muffins, 86

Mushrooms
Barley and Mushroom Cassserole, 128
Individual Winter Squash with Mushroom and Spinach Stuffing, 240
Mushroom and Hazelnut Snacking Balls, 133
Mushroom Pasta, 122
Pizza Casserole for Pesach, 249
Scrambled Mushrooms with Tofu and Curry, 115
Spinach/Mushroom Kugel, 250
Stuffed Mushrooms or Cherry Tomatoes, 140
Vegetable Stock, 177

Nuts (Almonds, Pecans, Walnuts, etc.)
A.M. Crunchies for Pesach, 251
Fruit and Nut Bread, 77
Mushroom and Hazelnut Snacking Balls, 133
Passover Toffee, 253

Oats (Old-Fashioned or Rolled)
Crunchy Granola, 74
Oatmeal for One, 199
Oatmeal for the Whole Crew, 199
Peanut Butter Oatmeal Cookie Bars, 62

Okra (Fresh or Frozen)
Okra Bayou, 166

Olives
Capanata, 194

Onion
Capanata, 194
Cilantro-Marinated Tofu or Tofurky, 242
Cucumber and Avocado Soup, 190
Pesach Stuffed Derma (Kishka), 248
Pizza Casserole for Pesach, 249
Potage Crecy, 179
Rice Casserole, 127
Russian Beet Borscht, 186
Spinach/Mushroom Kugel, 250
Southwestern-Influenced Rice and Pepper Medley, 112
Summer Squash and Eggplant Stew (Ratatouille), 119
Tofu Balls with Sauerkraut and Mustard, 132
Tomato Baked Beans, 60
Vegan Chopped Liver, 143
Vegan Kishka, 121
White Cupboard Chili, 111

Orange Juice
Dried Fruit Stew, 206
Sweet Potatoes in Orange Shells, 152

Oranges
Sweet Potatoes in Orange Shells, 152

Parsley
Spinach and Parsley Salad Dressing, 195

Pasta
Casserole with Uncooked Potatoes, 58
Microwave Lasagna, 116
Mixed Beans and Macaroni Casserole, 56
Mushroom Pasta, 122

Peaches (Canned)
Hot Sundaes, 70

Peanut Butter
Peanut Butter-Fudge Sauce, 73
Peanut Butter Oatmeal Cookie Bars, 62

Pears
A.M. Poached Pears, 212
Asian Spice, Asian Pear Salad with "Creamy" Apple Cider Dressing, 244

Peas (Frozen)
Peas with Mushrooms and Onions, 171

Pineapple (Canned)
Teenie Beenie Weenies, Updated, 124

Pinto Beans
Veggie Balls, 134

Potatoes
Baked Potatoes, 144
"Boiled" Potatoes, 145
Double Stuffed Green and Purple Potatoes, 238
Hot Potato and Caraway Salad (Vegan German Potato Salad), 150
Mashed Potatoes, 146
Mashed Potatoes with Rutabagas, 147
Pizza Potatoes, 149
Potato and Asparagus Vichyssoise (Cold Potato and Asparagus Soup), 188
Stuffed Baked Potatoes, 148
Vegan Sausage and Creamy Potatoes, 123
Vegetable-Corn Soup, 54

Prunes
Citrus Dried Plums, 208
Scandinavian Dried Fruit Dessert, 94
Spicy Dried Fruit Compote, 209

Pumpkin Purée
Creamy Pumpkin Soup, 184
Pumpkin Bread, 78
Pumpkin Custard, 69

Raisins
Asian Spice, Asian Pear Salad with "Creamy" Apple Cider Dressing, 244
Baked Raisins and Apricots, 211
Citrus Dried Plums, 208
Dried Fruit Stew, 206
Golden Carrots, 160
Raisin and Orange Cake, 81
Raisin Pie, 93
Southwestern-Influenced Rice and Pepper Medley, 112

Rhubarb
Rhubarb Sauce, 206
Stewed Fresh Rhubarb, 207

Rice
Creamy Garlic Rice with Parsley and Onions, 153
Fast "Fried" Rice, 125
Orange Rice with Celery, 151
Rice Casserole, 127
Rice for Breakfast, 204
Spanish-Style Rice, 126
Spinach Rice with Almonds, 154

Rice Cereal
Crispy Date Bars, 104

Romaine Lettuce
Asian Spice, Asian Pear Salad with "Creamy" Apple Cider Dressing, 244
Lemon-Parsley Apple and Cucumber Salad, 245

Rutabaga
Mashed Potatoes with Rutabagas, 147

Sauerkraut
Tofu Balls with Sauerkraut and Mustard, 132

Sausage, Vegan
Vegan Sausage and Creamy Potatoes, 123

Seeds (Pumpkin, Sunflower, etc.)
Crunchy Granola, 74

Seitan, Plain and Smoked
Casserole with Uncooked Potatoes, 58

Snow Peas
Orange Snow Peas with Cashews, 167
Snow Peas with Pine Nuts, 168

Sour Cream, Vegan
Spinach and Parsley Salad Dressing, 195

Soy Crumbles
Taco Salad, 113

Soy Yogurt
Make-Ahead Muffins, 88
Spinach and Parsley Salad Dressing, 195

Spinach (Fresh or Frozen)
Creamy Spinach, 155
Double Stuffed Green and Purple Potatoes, 238
Garlic Spinach with Sesame, 161
Individual Winter Squash with Mushroom and Spinach Stuffing, 240
Lemon-Parsley Apple and Cucumber Salad, 245
Spinach Lasagna, 118
Spinach/Mushroom Kugel, 250
Spinach and Parsley Salad Dressing, 195
Spinach Rice with Almonds, 154
Stuffed Mushrooms or Cherry Tomatoes, 140

Split Peas
Split Pea Soup, 53

Squash (Acorn, Crookneck or Yellow, Spaghetti Squash, Zucchini, etc.)
Cranberry Winter Squash, 159
Easy Zucchini, 172
Fresh Summer Squash Soup, 182
Individual Winter Squash with Mushroom and Spinach Stuffing, 240
Summer Squash and Eggplant Stew (Ratatouille), 119
Tri-Colored Stuffed Summer Squash, 59
Whole Spaghetti Squash, 173

Strawberries (Fresh or Frozen)
Stewed Fresh Rhubarb, 207
Strawberry Sauce, 72

Sweet Potatoes
Sweet Potato and Raisin Tzimmes, 252
Sweet Potatoes in Orange Shells, 152

Tofu (Plain or Smoked)
Apple Pie Tofu, 69
Broccoli and Cheese Soup, 180
Casserole with Uncooked Potatoes, 58
Cilantro-Marinated Tofu or Tofurky, 242
French Toast Matzo, 203
Hot and Sweet Tofu, 69
Make-Ahead Muffins, 88
Microwave Lasagna, 116
No-Bake Pumpkin Tofu Custard, 246
Scrambled Mushrooms with Tofu and Curry, 115
Spinach Lasagna, 118
Tofu Balls with Sauerkraut and Mustard, 132

Tofurky
Cilantro-Marinated Tofu or Tofurky, 242

Tomato Juice
Russian Beet Borscht, 186

Tomatoes
Stuffed Mushrooms or Cherry Tomatoes, 140
Stuffed Tomatoes Mediterranean, 114
Taco Salad, 113
Tomatoes Au Gratin, 212

Tomatoes (Canned)
Microwave Lasagna, 116
Mushroom Pasta, 122
Southwestern-Influenced Rice and Pepper Medley, 112
Summer Squash and Eggplant Stew (Ratatouille), 119
Vegetable-Corn Soup, 54

Tomato Sauce
Capanata, 194
Individual Microwave Pizzas, 142
Individual Winter Squash with Mushroom and Spinach Stuffing, 240
Microwave Lasagna, 116
Pizza Casserole for Pesach, 249
Pizza Potatoes, 149
Spanish-Style Rice, 126

Tortilla Chips
Spicy Toasted Nachos, 139
Taco Salad, 113

Vegetable Broth or Stock
Barley and Mushroom Cassserole, 128
Broccoli and Cheese Soup, 180
Bulgur Pilaf, 129
Cream of Cauliflower, 178
Creamy Pumpkin Soup, 184
Cucumber and Avocado Soup, 190
Fast Barley Soup, 183
Fast "Fried" Rice, 125
Fresh Summer Squash Soup, 182
Golden Carrots, 160
Green Steamed Kohlrabi, 163
Parsley and Soy Cauliflower, 158
Potage Crecy, 179
Red Pepper Soup, 185
Rice Casserole, 127
Savory Mushroom Gravy, 243
Spanish-Style Rice, 126
Vegetable Broth, 230
Vegetable Stock, 177
White Cupboard Chili, 111

Water Chestnuts
Mixed Beans and Macaroni Casserole, 56

Wheat Germ
Crunchy Granola, 74

White Beans
Tomato Baked Beans, 60
Vegetable-Corn Soup, 54
White Cupboard Chili, 111